school success
for kids with
High-Functioning
Autism

school success
for kids with
High-Functioning
Autism

Stephan M. Silverman, Ph.D.,
Lauren Kenworthy, Ph.D.,
& Rich Weinfeld

PRUFROCK PRESS INC.
WACO, TEXAS

Dedication

To our parents, Milton and Judith Silverman, Rosalind and Eldon Kenworthy, and Charles and Irene Weinfeld, who gave us the gift of the love of learning and always held high expectations for each of us.

We also would like to dedicate this book to our spouses, Karin Silverman, Eric Schaeffer, and Sara Shelley, in appreciation of their love, support, and patience that made this project possible.

Library of Congress Cataloging-in-Publication Data

Silverman, Stephan, 1942-
School success for kids with high-functioning autism / by Stephan M. Silverman, Ph.D.,
Lauren Kenworthy, Ph.D., & Rich Weinfeld.
    pages cm
Includes bibliographical references.
ISBN 978-1-61821-165-1 (pbk.)
1. Children with autism spectrum disorders--Education. I. Title.
LC4717.S56 2014
371.9--dc23
                        2013046407

Prufrock Press Inc.
P.O. Box 8813
Waco, TX 76714-8813
Phone: (800) 998-2208
Fax: (800) 240-0333
http://www.prufrock.com

Table of Contents

Acknowledgements

We would like to acknowledge Drs. Brenda Smith Myles, Taruna Ahluvalia, Annie McLaughlin, Marcy Jackson, Shawn Lattanzio, Dan Shapiro, Sabra Gelfond, and Bill McGrath for their insightful comments on this book. We would also like to express our gratitude to our editor, Lacy Compton.

We are grateful to Dr. Temple Grandin for taking the time review our book and provide a valuable foreword. She continues to lead and inspire both through her words and through her ongoing achievements.

We also would like to acknowledge the many families we have worked with, the school administrators and teachers we have had the privilege to collaborate with, and finally, the students with HFASD themselves, who provide us with daily inspiration.

Foreword

I really liked the way this book emphasized using the child's strengths and special interests to motivate schoolwork. My ability in art was always encouraged, and artistic skills formed the basis of my career designing livestock handling facilities. Half the cattle in the U.S. are handled in equipment I designed. Today I am a professor of animal science at Colorado State University. When I was a young child, I was totally nonverbal until age 4 and I had all of the behavioral symptoms of severe autism. When I was young, many people thought I was mentally retarded. Fortunately, I had a great early education program and both my mother and good teachers helped me to be successful.

Autism a Broad Spectrum

One of the difficulties in educating children with autism is that it is such a broad spectrum. Autism spectrum disorder (ASD) ranges from highly gifted individuals to individuals who remain nonverbal with severe handicaps. I have observed problems with some teachers not being able to "shift gears" between teaching a highly gifted child on the autism spectrum and teaching a nonverbal child with intellectual disabilities. Kids on the high end of the autism spectrum often have uneven skills. They may be gifted in one subject and be below grade level in another subject. I am a visual thinker and all my thoughts are in pictures. This made learning algebra impossible. Another cognitive type, which may occur on the autism spectrum, is the mathematical pattern thinker who is good at math and may have problems with reading. A third type is a verbal thinker who is good at writing. The scientific studies that provide evidence for these different types of thinkers are reviewed in my book *The Autistic Brain*.

Bust Down the Boundaries Formed by Labels

I go to many conferences and work in industry with many different people. During my career, I have traveled back and forth between the livestock technical world, the autism world, and the gifted child world. From my experiences, I have learned that there is little communication between these worlds. There is a huge need to bust down the silos between the different groups to help bright kids who are different to succeed. When I go to a gifted conference, I see the same little geeky kids that I see at an autism conference. When I visit Silicon Valley, I see undiagnosed people with high-functioning autism or Asperger's working at high-paying jobs. At the meat plant, I have seen many undiagnosed people working in the maintenance department.

They were saved by taking welding, auto mechanics, or carpentry in high school. I think it is terrible that many schools have stopped teaching these hands-on classes. Unfortunately, I see too many gifted kids getting an autism label and they end up getting addicted to video games and unable to hold a job. This happens because they became their label and there are not enough expectations for achievement.

Direct Fixations Into Careers

Kids with autism often become fixated on their favorite things. Too often, I am seeing bright kids who get fixated on their autism diagnosis instead of getting fixated on something they could turn into a career, such as astronomy, math, drama, art, or science. To get kids fixated on useful things that could be shaped into a career requires exposing them to interesting things. In high school, I got fixated on building an Ames distorted room optical illusion after I viewed it in a science movie. This was beautifully shown in the HBO movie about my life. My high school science teacher was a great mentor who got me turned around and interested in studying.

Parents and teachers need to expose kids to lots of interesting activities and studies that can lead into a career, such as computer programming, art, and building things. TV watching and video game playing needs to be limited to one hour a day and the virtual computer world needs to get connected back to the real world. One resourceful mom took her son's fixation on the video game Minecraft and made real wood "Minecraft" blocks for her son and the neighborhood kids to play with. This provided a connection between building things in the virtual world and building structures in the real world. This also provided socialization with other children through a shared Minecraft interest. We must *not* let kids become recluses in their rooms.

When I was tortured in high school with teasing, shared special interests were refuges from bullies. My science teacher had a model rocket club, and I was an avid builder of rockets. There was no teasing during model rocket activities. The kids that did the teasing were not interested in rockets. All my friends in high school engaged in the same special interests of horseback riding, model rockets, and electronics. Educators need to get kids involved with making things. We had to build all our rockets. I was horrified to see an advertisement for prebuilt rockets. Designing, building, and testing a rocket for stability teaches practical problem solving.

Teaching Work Skills

Teaching work skills needs to start way before kids graduate from high school. I am seeing too many kids graduating from high school with no work skills. Learning work skills should start with having elementary school kids do household chores. Too often, parents overprotect a child who is labeled with autism spectrum disorder. Parents need to "stretch" these kids and teach basic skills such as shaking hands, crossing a road safely, and table manners. I like the term "stretch" because you need to move them just outside their comfort zones in order for them to develop. There should be no sudden surprises because that causes panic.

Kids should start jobs outside the home in middle school. I am going to call these jobs "paper route substitutes." Kids need to learn the responsibility and discipline of having a job. When I was 13, my mother set up a hand-sewing job I did for a freelance seamstress who worked out of her home. Other jobs that can be easily set up in the neighborhood are walking dogs for neighbors, volunteering at a farmer's market, fixing computers, making PowerPoints for a friend who is a business executive, or volunteering to set up and take down the chairs every weekend at the church. When kids are 16, they should get some experience in the regular job market and work a part-time job bagging groceries or working at McDonald's. If it is possible to get a career-related job, that would be even better. In Silicon Valley, many parents "apprentice" their child into computer programming and teach them their skills. By the time I graduated from high school, I had lots of work experience. I cleaned eight horse stalls every day and took care of the horse barn at my school. I did carpentry work and painted signs. During the summer I visited my aunt's ranch and built a gate that could be opened from a car, took guests on horseback rides, and waited on a few tables. In college, I did two volunteer internships. In one internship, I rented a house with another lady and worked in a research lab. At another internship, I was a summer counselor in a program for kids with autism. All of my job experiences were set up by my mother and the college through local contacts.

In conclusion, I want to see talented, gifted kids who are on the autism spectrum succeed. Don't get stuck on the label. Emphasize what the child *can do*, not what he or she *cannot do*. Build on the area of strength and get kids involved in lots of interesting activities they can enjoy with peers with similar interests. Einstein had no language until age 3. In many school systems, he would be labeled autism spectrum disorder (ASD). What would happen to little Albert today? In some schools, he would have gone down the wrong path. Both parents and teachers need to work together and always make sure they see the child and not the label.

Temple Grandin, Ph.D.
Professor of Animal Science
Colorado State University

Introduction

Stanley, 13, was sitting at the dinner table across from his grandfather. The table had been cleared and the family had moved to the den to watch a football game. As usual on such evenings, Grandpa engaged Stanley in his favorite topic of interest—Vietnam War history. Grandpa served in the infantry in Vietnam and was trying to get a word in edgewise from his memory about a particular campaign, but Stanley was going on and on about the very battle in which Grandpa fought. Finally, Grandpa interrupted Stanley to correct a factual detail. Apparently, Stanley had incorrectly identified the name of the commanding officer on a specific day of the conflict. Even though he took part in the battle, Grandpa's memory was shaky. He thought he was right. Stanley went to his room and pulled out a reference book. Stanley was right! There didn't seem to be anything Stanley didn't know about the war. He continued to reel off fact after fact in a determined, but emotionless, monotone, hardly looking toward his grandfather's face the whole time. Grandpa wanted to share stories of the friends he made and lost in the war, the emotions he felt, and the human drama he experienced, but Stanley seemed only interested in tactical facts and the names of armaments and generals. Grandpa wasn't sure that what he thought, knew, or remembered about the war really mattered to Stanley. They weren't really connecting. Stanley, like thousands of other children, has high-functioning autism spectrum disorder or HFASD.

This book is written for parents, educators, and other professionals who are concerned with providing an education to children like Stanley. It focuses on providing practical strategies that can be used by parents and classroom teachers and summarizes relevant research in the ever-expanding field of the education of students with HFASD. Because a fully detailed review of research is beyond the scope of this book, we encourage interested readers to refer to the works of the leaders in this field, including Drs. Hans Asperger, Tony Attwood, Simon Baron-Cohen, Mohammad Ghaziuddin, Christopher Gillberg, Ami Klin, Brenda Smith Myles, Uta Frith, Sally Ozonoff, Michael Powers, Fred R. Volkmar, and Lorna Wing. If we have omitted the recognition of other pivotal individuals in this area of research and application of knowledge, we apologize. Very few researchers have directly addressed the wide variety of issues involved in general and special education for students with HFASD. A few notable exceptions in the literature are Drs. Attwood, Ozonoff, Baron-Cohen, Klin, Myles, and Volkmar. Their work, along with that of others, will be discussed briefly in relation to the education of students with HFASD and what was formerly termed Asperger's syndrome in the chapters that follow.

HFASD should be recognized as early possible in the developing child. Not only do we hope that the diagnosis will be applied as early as possible and with accuracy, but we hope that the strengths of each child with HFASD are understood and supported in the educational environment. It is very encouraging that early identification and early intervention have been increasingly recognized in the literature, especially in clinical and educational practice.

The educational experience for children like Stanley should support their zeal and intellectual ability so that learning can be as joyful and productive as the experience is for other children. Children are all born wanting to learn, and the experience of learning should be a happy one—starting with early development until the young person becomes a productive member of society. Because HFASD is an autism spectrum disorder, not just a developmental difference or aggregate of eccentricities, children with HFASD will, at some time in their educational careers, need special approaches to education. Special education may not be required in every subject area and skill domain. To whatever extent possible, the child with HFASD should have learning experiences that work for more typically developing children, as long as he or she is deriving meaningful benefit from these learning opportunities and is able to access the curriculum.

This is more than a second edition of *School Success for Kids With Asperger's Syndrome* (Silverman & Weinfeld, 2007). It is very much a new book. Since late 2006, when *School Success for Kids With Asperger's Syndrome* was first published, new information has emerged on every front. This includes knowledge of genetics, the brain, better assessment techniques, and the awareness of the needs of the college student and working adult with HFASD. There still remains the need for more evidence-based treatment and instructional interventions. Lauren Kenworthy, Director of the Center for Autism Spectrum Disorders, Children's National Medical Center, has joined the authorship team to integrate the latest research findings on the causes and treatment of HFASD.

The focus of this book is not only to accept and affirm the humanity of children with HFASD and aid them in obtaining their right to an education that is consistent with typical development, but also to "fill in the gaps" where their special needs hamper their ability to access instruction and progress in knowledge. As for children with any disability, the definition of a disability implies the need for additional support in educational areas. There is also a set of instructional strategies and targeted skill areas beyond the curriculum that require emphasis in order for children with HFASD to function in a complex and competitive world. We will discuss these strategies and skill areas later in the book.

This book is about the special opportunities to enhance learning for children with HFASD in accommodating for and instructing them in their areas of need, while celebrating and nurturing their special skills. We hope to provide functional guidelines for teachers who have these children in their charge. The first half of this book is a general survey of HFASD with an attempt to highlight critical issues in diagnosis, treatment, and education. Keep in mind as you are reading this book that not all of the information available on HFASD could be included in a short reference book like this one. We are at an early point in the history of this field and at the beginning of an explosion of critically important new research. You will want to seek out other resources as you begin to understand your child's or student's disorder, including books, websites, and other resources. Many such resources are listed in Appendix A. The second half of the book focuses entirely on interventions for children and young adults with HFASD (with additional tools in Appendices B–E). These include best practices for working with these students in the classroom, as well as tips for parents on how to navigate the school system to provide the best fit for their child and advice for supporting their child's learning at home. Every child is unique, and therefore, has different needs in and out of the classroom. Some of our suggestions may help more than others, but we hope you find something in this book that you can take to your child's teacher or that you can use in your own classroom with your students who have HFASD. We also provide a menu of placement and instructional options to think about as you work with the educational system.

Although there is no cure for HFASD, this book hopes to provide some preventative interventions and early supports to circumvent long-term negative effects of the condition. We hope this book helps to support each child in reaching his or her potential and having a successful educational experience. Today, educators and parents need to work with what information we have in making practical and effective daily decisions. We hope this book will help you help the child in your life with HFASD succeed in school and beyond.

chapter 1

What Are High-Functioning Autism Spectrum Disorders?

Being eccentric or unusual has become increasingly more acceptable. From the awkwardly entertaining character of Sheldon on the TV show *The Big Bang Theory*, to the increasing appearance of bookish personalities in all aspects of popular culture, we are becoming more comfortable with members of our community who were seen in recent times as odd. Recently, the word *geek*, initially a derogatory term, has become a humorous, culturally descriptive term for persons who are far more interested intellectually in technical data and activities than they are skilled in working with people. Now there are computer consultation groups and individuals who rent out their services, such as Best Buy's "Geek Squad."

Pictured wearing pocket protectors and heavy horn-rimmed glasses, these same people were called "nerds" just one or two decades previously. When technology was somewhat less sophisticated, these same individuals sported slide rules in leather pouches on their belts. This image of the socially inept "techie" refers to a continuum of persons who lack the ability to read social cues or manage complex relationships, including the complex Western game of dating.

More recently, it has been suggested that social skill deficits are more than a difference or an eccentricity—they can fall into a disability classification requiring special supports. This occurs when the so-called "geekiness" shares characteristics of high-functioning autism spectrum disorder, which has also been called Asperger's syndrome. In fact, there are lots of different terms that have been applied to this group. In this book, we will generally use the term HFASD to capture both the autism symptoms and the strong intellectual abilities of this group. When referring to all individuals with autism, we will use the abbreviation ASD and when referring to specific past studies or investigations conducted with children identified as having Asperger's syndrome, we will use that term. In brief, HFASD is characterized by poor social skills, inflexibility, and overfocused interests, which can occur despite normal intelligence, vocabulary, and grammar skills. Hans Asperger, the Viennese psychiatrist who first identified this disorder, described "little professors" who could be highly successful professionally and had a lot to offer society, but needed specialized education to succeed.

History of HFASD

In order to better understand children with HFASD, it's helpful to know some of the history behind the discovery of Asperger's syndrome as a disorder and the research and treatment that has followed. The term *autism* was first used by Dr. Eugen Bleuler (1857–1939) to identify extreme egocentrism or a shutting off of relations between the individual and others. The discovery of the group of people we now consider as having HFASD is attributed to Hans Asperger (1906–1980), who, after working with hundreds of children, reported on a study of four boys, ages 6 to 11, in Vienna in 1944. Asperger identified a pattern of behavior and abilities in these boys that he originally called "autistic personality disorders in childhood," and later referred to as "autistic psychopathy," meaning "self-personality disease." Autistic psychopathy was for Asperger a constitutionally given personality type. He noted that almost all of the children were boys and all had at least one parent, usually the father, with a similar, but less extreme, set of traits. Asperger (1944) observed the following traits: little ability to form friendships, conversation that was one-sided, intense absorption in a special interest, and clumsy physical movements.

Asperger developed a strengths model of the children, whom he identified in this group as having "autistic psychopathy" (Frith, 1991). He deemphasized their weaknesses, believing that their strengths would carry into adulthood. One example he noted was a child named Fritz V. True to Asperger's expectations, Fritz did manifest his strengths into adulthood and became a professor of astronomy, solving an error in Newton's work that Fritz first had discovered as a child. Asperger was a pioneer in the education of his subjects, opening a school for this group of children near the end of World War II. Sadly, the school was bombed and demolished. This may have contributed to further delays in the spread of Asperger's findings, as much of his work was destroyed.

It has been speculated that Asperger may have possessed aspects of the condition later named after him by Lorna Wing, a British researcher. He himself was an isolated child who found it difficult to make friends. He had a seemingly obsessive interest in an Austrian poet, and he repeatedly recited passages from the poet's works to his classmates, who did not share his enthusiasm for the material.

Asperger wrote in German and his work was not frequently translated into other languages. It was not until the publication of "Asperger's Syndrome: A Clinical Account" in 1981 by Wing in the journal *Psychological Medicine* that Asperger's work was widely known in the United States. Wing's study of 35 individuals aged 5–35 introduced Asperger's work to the English-speaking world. In her paper, Wing dropped the term autistic psychopathy, because it was seen as stigmatizing and suggestive of voluntary antisocial actions in the individuals described by the label. In 1991, Asperger's work was translated into English 47 years after his original publication.

Dr. Leo Kanner, often referred to as the father of child psychiatry, was working with children on the autism spectrum at Johns Hopkins University in Baltimore, MD, around the same time Asperger was conducting his study. Kanner and Asperger initially had no knowledge of each other and, when they did, they corresponded briefly, but believed that they were working with two very different kinds of children. Kanner's subjects were more severe, with a broader range of symptoms, and often were less verbal and had lower IQ scores than those children described by Asperger. Kanner first described the children he was working with as having "autistic disturbances of affective contact" (1943), which he later referred to as early infantile autism (Kanner & Eisenberg, 1956). Kanner placed autism within the categories of schizophrenia, and other psychoanalysts most frequently attributed the cause, although unknown, to "refrigerator" mothers who lacked the ability to demonstrate affection to their children and who may have, consciously or unconsciously, been rejecting them. During this time, parents not only had to adjust to the challenge of rearing a child with autism, they also were made to feel guilty that their child's disabilities were the result of poor parenting.

Whereas Asperger's work received little attention before the 1980s, Kanner's work became accepted internationally, and autism was generally thought to be an emotional disturbance related to schizophrenia or a form of intellectual disability. Consequently, until the 1980s, children were usually not considered to have autism unless they also had deficits in intelligence and language skills. Over the last several decades there has been a growing awareness both of the biological causes of autism (genes and brain differences) and of the wide spectrum of language and intellectual abilities that people with autism can have. These changes had a major impact on the rules for diagnosing autism in the mental health practitioner's guidebook, the American Psychiatric Association's *Diagnostic and Statistical Manual of Mental Disorders* (DSM), the fourth edition of which was published in 1994 (and had a text revision in 2000). The DSM-IV introduced the diagnosis of Asperger's syndrome, and the idea that a person could have high-functioning autism gained traction. Asperger's syndrome and high-functioning autism were thought to be two distinct disorders, both characterized by normal intelligence, social skills problems, and repetitive behaviors, but distinguished from each other based on language development. Basic language skills (vocabulary, grammar, understanding) were considered intact in Asperger's syndrome throughout development, but impaired in high-functioning autism. However, studies conducted throughout the 1990s and early 2000s generally failed to find a meaningful difference between the two conditions as they were defined in the DSM-IV (Happé, 2011). Furthermore, different, well-respected autism clinics across the nation did not make the diagnoses in a consistent manner. Even when using gold standard diagnostic tests, different clinics and autism teams came to different conclusions about who had high-functioning autism and who had Asperger's syndrome (Lord et al, 2012).

How Are Autism Spectrum Disorders Currently Defined?

In order to address these problems, the newest diagnostic guidelines, just published as the fifth edition of the *Diagnostic and Statistical Manual of Mental Disorders* (DSM-5; APA, 2013), have removed the different subcategories within autism, including Asperger's syndrome and Pervasive Developmental Disorder, Not Otherwise Specified. Now clinicians are instructed to make one diagnosis, autism spectrum disorder, for all people who have problems with social communication and social interaction, and have restricted, repetitive, and inflexible behaviors. The diagnosis of ASD is then qualified by a description of language abilities and intelligence. For example, a person who previously received an Asperger's diagnosis would probably be diagnosed with ASD "without accompanying intellectual or language impairment." This simplification makes sense because the previous subcategories of autism, such as Asperger's, were not clearly defined or consistently applied. The rules for distinguishing Asperger's syndrome from autism were unclear, so that even the most careful clinicians in different clinics could give the same child different diagnoses. It is also an improvement because it releases diagnosticians from imposing categorical distinctions such as Asperger's versus high-functioning autism on a disorder that occurs on a spectrum as opposed to in discrete categories (Constantino & Todd, 2003; Szatmari, 2000).

On the other hand, it is confusing and upsetting for a lot of people who have grown up with the Asperger's diagnosis, attended Asperger's school programs, and made friends on Asperger's-related social networks to suddenly have this term removed. It is important that high-functioning individuals with an autism spectrum disorder and their families are able to use the term that they think fits best, and many families and programs may continue to use the term Asperger's syndrome. For the purposes of clarity, however, this book refers to autism spectrum disorders (ASD) generally and high-functioning autism spectrum disorder (HFASD) specifically to indicate the presence of social deficits and repetitive, inflexible behaviors in a person with normal or high intelligence and good basic vocabulary, sentence structure, and comprehension of language.

To complicate matters further, the most recent diagnostic guidelines (APA, 2013) also introduced a new language disorder: Social Communication Disorder. It describes people with similar social communication problems and social reciprocity deficits as are seen in ASD, but without repetitive, inflexible behaviors. Recommendations and treatments suggested in this book and elsewhere for HFASD that target social issues may also be appropriate for people diagnosed with Social Communication Disorder. On the other hand, those targeting inflexibility should not be needed for a person with Social Communication Disorder, if that diagnosis has been accurately made.

Another change in the diagnostic rules is that clinicians are now allowed to make a diagnosis of Attention Deficit/Hyperactivity Disorder (ADHD) in a person who is also diagnosed with an ASD. In the DSM-IV, that was not technically allowed. This is a major improvement, because about one third of children with HFASD also have ADHD, and more than half of children with HFASD have problems with attention and impulse control even if they don't meet the full criteria for ADHD (Leyfer et al., 2006). The presence of ADHD symptoms in addition to ASD means that specific accommodations and treatments for attention and impulse control may be helpful in addition to the accommodations and treatments suggested for the social communication and flexibility problems associated with ASD.

How Do Schools Define Autism Spectrum Disorders?

As you will read below, many of the important interventions and treatments for HFASD occur in schools. Separate from a clinical diagnosis, students must be identified with an educational disability in order to qualify for special education services. This identification is governed by federal law in the Individuals with Disabilities Education Act (IDEA) of 1990, which was revised in 1997 and 2004. This law and its ramifications will be discussed in detail in Chapter 7. School districts only have one special education eligibility classification available for autistic spectrum disorder, so the recent changes in clinical diagnostic rules may not change how schools define autism for the purposes of special education. There is a risk, however, that some students who would have previously received a clinical ASD diagnosis and educational autism disability classification, could now be given a Social Communication Disorder diagnosis and the educational classification of a speech/language disability.

How Common Are Autism Spectrum Disorders?

The Centers for Disease Control and Prevention (CDC, n.d.) launched the Autism and Developmental Disabilities Monitoring Network in 2000, which aims to get the most accurate statistics possible on the prevalence of ASD by collecting information on thousands of children from schools, medical clinics, and social service providers. The CDC has reported a 78% increase in ASD between 2002–2008, and that between 1%–2% of children in the United States has autism or a closely related disorder (CDC, 2012). It is important to understand that this estimate is based on a survey of only 14 U.S. states and may not reflect the true prevalence of autism because the CDC count is not based on in-person clinical exams but on expert review of school and clinical reports for key words that suggest a diagnosis of ASD. Even with these caveats, it is clear that autism is an urgent public health issue and a major concern, as reported by Dr. Yeargin-Allsopp, chief of the developmental disabilities branch of the CDC (n.d.). The most recent CDC findings indicate that five times as many boys are affected by ASD as girls and the majority (62%) of children identified with ASD do not have intellectual disability. Although more White than Black or Hispanic children are identified as having ASD, this is thought to reflect underidentification in minority groups related to lack of services instead of a true difference in prevalence (CDC, 2012; Durkin et al., 2010).

One of the most prominent questions surrounding ASD at this time is: "Is there really a rise in the disorder's occurrence and, if so, why?" The answer turns out to be complex and not yet fully understood. There was an almost tenfold increase in measured prevalence of ASDs throughout the 1980s and 1990s (see Fombonne, 2003, for a review) that appears to have been primarily related to increases in awareness of autism and expansion in the types of children who received the ASD diagnosis. As more high-functioning children were identified as having ASD, and some lower functioning children were shifted from intellectual disability to autism classifications, it was only natural for the total number of children diagnosed with autism to increase. Furthermore, as more pediatricians, therapists, teachers, and parents became aware of autism as a result of expanding autism screening requirements, news coverage, and research, more children were referred for and received autism diagnoses. From this perspective, the increasing prevalence of ASD is a good thing because it means that more children who have ASD are getting identified and receiving treatment.

As the numbers of children diagnosed with ASD have continued to rise, however, speculation has spread through the popular press about an "epidemic" of ASD. Although it is not an epidemic in the sense of malaria or polio, some scientists do believe that there actually are increasing numbers of cases of ASD, as opposed to just better identification of those who have the disorder. A variety of explanations are offered for why this might be happening. Some point to population centers where high-tech communities have arisen (e.g., Silicon Valley) and where "geeks" marry "geeks," and give birth to increasing numbers of children who have ASD. Dr. Simon Baron-Cohen has hypothesized that people with systemizing brains are finding each other and creating a genetic predisposition toward producing higher rates of HFASD in their offspring (Morton, 2001). Others researchers emphasize social trends, such as older parents having children, which can increase the risk of having children with autism (Hultman, Sandin, Levine, Lichtenstein, & Reichenberg, 2010). Regardless of the cause, there are more children now than ever before who are diagnosed with ASD. This has caused school systems to adjust rapidly to implement effective supports and interventions for these students.

What Causes Autism Spectrum Disorders?

Autism is highly heritable, as demonstrated by the fact that if one monozygotic (identical) twin has ASD, then his or her twin has a very strong chance of also having ASD (Geschwind, 2011). Because heritability is much lower in dizygotic (fraternal) twins, who do not share exactly the same genes like monozygotic twins do, we know that there is a very strong genetic influence in ASD. That does not mean that there is a simple genetic abnormality that is identified as causing all, or even most, cases of ASD. One of the striking aspects of ASDs is how different, or heterogeneous, people with ASD are. For example, there is no other developmental disorder in which intelligence routinely ranges from profoundly impaired to very superior, or in which language abilities range from no verbal ability to the remarkable verbal gifts of writers like John Elder Robison. Hence the popularity of this statement, made by self-advocate and university professor Stephen Shore, at a conference once: "If you've met one person with autism, you've met one person with autism." The variability in presentation of ASD is also reflected in its etiology, or what causes it. Some scientists talk about the "autisms" to emphasize that there may be different disorders with different biological profiles that we are lumping together as ASD. Only about 10% of children who are diagnosed with an ASD have a known genetic syndrome, like Fragile X, or tuberous sclerosis (Zafeiriou, Ververi, Dafoulis, Kalyva, &Vargiami, 2013). For all of the other cases of ASD, the genetic contribution is much more complicated. There are more than 200 genes that can contribute to the risk of having autism, but which particular genes are related to autism in a particular individual is variable (Persico & Napolioni, 2013). In many cases, there are a number of genes that interact to cause the disorder. So there is no simple pattern of inheritance like that taught in high school biology regarding eye color. Further complicating the situation is that some genetic defects in ASD are not passed from parent to child but occur as spontaneous changes in the child.

The next layer of complexity is related to the fact that some genes only seem to cause autism when specific environmental or nongenetic events occur. To end up with ASD, a person often needs both a genetic vulnerability or risk and a piece of bad luck in the form of an exposure of some kind. Some of the environmental factors that have been shown to increase the risk of autism are: maternal infection during pregnancy (Zerbo et al., 2013); maternal drug use during pregnancy, especially the antiseizure medicine valproate (Christensen et al., 2013); exposure to pesticides as they are sprayed on crops (Shelton, Hertz-Picciotto, & Pessah, 2012); and other air pollutants (Roberts et al., 2013).

Although there is still a lot to be understood regarding the causes of autism, we do know that, through a combination of genetic abnormalities and environmental events, the brains of people diagnosed with ASD become different from those of the average person. Here again the variability and complexity of what causes ASD and how ASD is expressed limits definitive findings, but the evidence is accumulating that the synapses, or links between neurons in the brain, are altered in ASD, and that there are less effective connections between different parts of the brains of people with ASD (Dennis & Thompson, 2013). The social-communication and behavioral flexibility skills that are impaired in autism rely on especially complex, interconnected networks of neurons in the brain. It is not one simple part of the brain or one set of neurons that enables a person to notice sarcasm in another person's voice or manage an unexpected situation effectively. By using functional magnetic resonance imaging (fMRI) to observe how people's brains react to social and flexibility demands, scientists have clearly demonstrated that the interconnected networks typical people use do not respond in the same way for people with ASD (Dichter, 2012).

For example, when Schultz and colleagues (2000) showed pictures of faces to people with autism, they found little activation in a face processing area called the fusiform face area (FFA), but did find a high level of activity in a nearby brain region associated with recognizing objects. Critchley et al. (2000) also found a failure to activate regions in the face processing area when appraising emotional facial expressions. When looking for relationships between moving geometric shapes and brain areas, Schultz and colleagues (2000) found that social-like cooperative movements between the shapes correlated with activity in the FFA, leading them to determine that the FFA may not only deal with recognizing faces, but also with recognizing perceptions and interactions that are social in nature. They refer to the "social brain" as the interconnected network of brain regions that includes the amygdala, the medial frontal cortex, the superior temporal sulcus, and the FFA (Schultz et al., 2000).

Although there are not yet definitive answers about what causes most cases of ASD, there has been progress in our understanding. We have determined that it is a biologically based disorder of the brain that results in differences in the way people with ASD understand and process social information and regulate their behavior. We know that genes, both what is inherited from parents and how genes are expressed in children with ASD, play a major but not exclusive role in causing these differences. Perhaps most importantly, although we know that the environment affects brain development, we have stopped barking up some very wrong trees: We no longer blame parents or vaccines (Fombonne, Zakarian, Bennett, Meng, & McLean-Heywood, 2006) for causing autism, and this in itself is a triumph of science.

What Can We Expect for a Child With HFASD?

Just as the presentation of people with ASD is variable, so are their outcomes. A small number of people diagnosed with ASD in childhood make such large gains as they grow that they may no longer have enough problems to qualify for an ASD diagnosis, although they still experience challenges in various related areas (Fein et al., 2013). There are also people with HFASD who struggle to live independently, maintain a relationship, or hold down a job (Farley et al., 2009; Howlin & Moss, 2012; Smith, Maenner, & Seltzer, 2012; Taylor & Seltzer, 2010). Poorer outcome is generally associated with a lack of functional language by 5 years of age, intellectual disability, greater severity of social deficits, seizures, and psychiatric problems. One of the strongest motivations for identifying people with HFASD at an early age is that, without specific supports and teaching, even highly gifted individuals who have a lot to offer society and a genuine desire to make a contribution are prevented from doing so by their social and behavioral problems. On the other hand, many people with HFASD are able to make major gains when intensive, early intervention is provided.

A Final Note About the Use and Misuse of Labels

Because of the rise in interest in ASD, we must guard against overinclusion in the classification. Not every exceptionally gifted person and not every socially inept person has HFASD. A profound interest or passion in a topic or activity does not in itself qualify one as disabled. An ASD diagnosis is only properly made when a person is experiencing "clinically significant impairment in social, occupational, or other important areas of current functioning" (APA, 2013, p. 50). Without impairment there should be no diagnosis. When, however, are the "little professors" more than just intellectually top-heavy and when are they disabled? When the intense interests of the individual become obsessive and interfering and social interaction with others is frequently ineffective, the observer may be looking at a form of autism. The critical element is the lack of interest or ability to form satisfactory relationships and to engage in the rich interplay of language and emotional communication valued in our modern society.

It is also important to recognize that having a diagnosis of ASD brings with it key strengths that are needed by society. In her lectures, Temple Grandin, an accomplished scientist, author, professor, and internationally known spokesperson for persons with ASD, argues that as a society we would have experienced a great loss if Thomas Edison were chatting away constantly in social activities instead of persevering in inventing many of our modern conveniences. Its tolerance of diversity is a measure of how advanced a society is. Neurodiversity is one of the newest frontiers in the evolution of our society. Neurodiversity is just like other forms of diversity, and valuing diversity means that we value and include all kinds of minds in our society. Neurodiversity brings with it the same opportunities as religious, cultural, or racial diversity in terms of exposing us to new ways of thinking and solving problems and giving everyone a chance to contribute to society. To the extent that we can embrace and learn from people with ASD, we will all benefit.

chapter 2

How Might HFASD Appear to Parents and Teachers?

At first, Jack's parents were so excited and proud. He was reading books before the age of 4. It was clear he was a chip off the old block, as bright as his parents, one a Yale graduate and one a Columbia graduate. It was true that he was a little clumsy and his speech was a little delayed, but initially his parents could focus on how incredibly bright he appeared. Over time, however, his talent and interest in reading became an area of concern. Reading was all he wanted to do. As the other children played with one another, he would sit off to the side with his books. In preschool, his problems interacting socially quickly became evident. Jack was either uninterested in the other kids or when he did want someone's attention, he was more likely to push them than to speak to them. When his teachers would try to engage him, he would not make eye contact with them. The feeling of pride and expectation that his parents had initially felt was now tempered by doubt and fear.

There are many aspects of the developing child that emerge as challenges for parents and teachers. In this chapter, we hope to emphasize pivotal developmental concerns that may arise, and also the unique strengths observed during the development of children with HFASD. We have organized this chapter into categories reflecting the most common areas of difference in cognitive and behavioral development seen in children with HFASD.

Social Skills and Social Understanding

Social Engagement and Reciprocity

The primary characteristic of HFASD is the problem of human connectedness. The clinical term most commonly used to describe human connection is *reciprocity*. This refers to the individual's ability to engage other people in a way that makes everyone feel connected. Social delays and poor reciprocity related to HFASD are often observable in the first 2 years of life. Some babies with HFASD show less-than-expected interest and pleasure in other people. A child with HFASD may exhibit less eye contact with others than expected, and he or she may not read faces for cues about feelings or consequences. This lack of connectivity is often felt in an intangible way, especially by caregivers. For example, a child might not seem to want a parent's comfort when something bad has happened, or know how to comfort a sad or sick sibling. Children with HFASD might have difficulty showing that they appreciate a parent or teacher's help or that their praise makes them feel good. A pivotal skill for social interaction that is very often late to develop in babies with HFASD is joint attention. Joint attention is a normal, spontaneously occurring behavior in typical development whereby the infant shows enjoyment in sharing an object (or event) with another person by looking back and forth between the two. For example, if you point out an airplane in the sky, the baby looks at the airplane and then back at you with a smile, to share the pleasure of seeing it. This skill is at the core of social reciprocity.

We anticipate that a child will "give back" our attention. However, in children with HFASD, there may be less variation in expressions of emotions and joy in playing interactive games. The child's social smile may occur later in development and infrequently. Children with HFASD tend to be better attached to their parents than children with classical autism, and parents may not notice problems in parent-child interactions. But a child with HFASD will often have difficulty connecting with peers. Later in childhood, she may be more likely to engage (although often in a one-way conversation) with adults than with peers.

Play

Play is how young children learn and express social communication skills. The child with HFASD's play may be unusual. Instead of actively inventing new games and make-believe, he may prefer lining up toys, doing puzzles, building things, or drawing. He may not pretend or make up characters and give them dialogue like typical 4- and 5-year-olds do when playing house, superheroes, or other games. Play may also tend to be less creative and flexible: Specific scripts or routines may be repeated over and over, or the child may struggle to respond to new ideas and suggestions from peers and seek instead to control the play.

What psychologists call *parallel play* seems extended in the development of children with HFASD. In parallel play, children might enjoy playing with toys near each other, but they don't interact in sharing toys or games with each other. The child with HFASD may play a game with others, but will not initiate the opportunity. She may require coaxing, prodding, or encouragement to maintain participation in games or group activities.

Social Motivation

Social motivation is the natural pleasure a person gets from engaging with others. There is a wide spectrum of social motivation in typical people. Some of us love nothing better than a big party and may have trouble with long periods of solitude. Others get energy from being on our own, and although we value relationships with others, we may have just a few very good friends. In HFASD, social motivation is often but not always low, partly because interacting socially is confusing and has resulted in bad experiences in the past. Low social motivation does not mean that a person does not care about others. Many people with HFASD are altruistic and deeply loyal to their friends and family, but if you ask what makes them happy they may name their favorite computer game or special topic of interest instead of being with family and friends. Young children with HFASD may not express an interest in play dates. Often social motivation increases in a person with HFASD as he or she gets older. Whereas a primary school age child may not seem to notice that she doesn't have many friends, it may really bother a middle school age child with HFASD that she is having trouble making friends.

Social Understanding

Children with HFASD have a social learning disability. Just as a child with a reading disability has trouble making sense of written text, children with HFASD struggle to make sense of and express themselves through facial expression, body language, tone of voice, etc. The person with HFASD may not be able to read subtle gestures and facial changes or to interpret subtleties in language such as irony or sarcasm. She can seem stiff or stilted in her social interactions. In addition, the ability to make good judgments using the information obtained from "reading" others is limited. Johnson (2004) suggested that social deficits may be due to a lack of integration among various perceptual and intellectual abilities, as well as social understanding, memory, or recall. This can lead to social faux pas and means that children with HFASD need explicit step-by-step help dissecting, understanding, and correcting what went wrong in a social interchange.

A child with HFASD may seem narcissistically concerned with his own needs. This is related to another gap in social understanding in many people with HFASD called *theory of mind*, or the ability to understand that others have their own point of view and thoughts, feelings, and priorities. Theory of mind involves the ability to attribute mental states to others or to be able to intuit what others might be feeling in a given situation. Some researchers believe that the ability to guess others' states of mind is related to one's ability to effectively practice introspection on one's own. This suggests that the ability to know one's self in some way may relate to our skill in attributing feelings and motivations to others. Like everything else, the level of impairment in theory of mind is variable in HFASD. Individuals with more severe ASD may lack theory of mind altogether, while people with HFASD may be able to discern what others are thinking if they work at it. Williams (2004) suggested that, at the very least, people with ASD must work harder at theorizing what others are experiencing than most persons. Klin and colleagues (2003) emphasized that although people with HFASD might be able to figure out what a person is thinking if explicitly asked, social information is not automatically salient to, or noticed by, people with HFASD the way it is for typical people. Because of these deficits, people with HFASD may interpret statements by others in an overly concrete and literal fashion (Kaland et al., 2002). This means that children with HFASD need more prompt questions and more time than others to understand social subtleties in language, such as irony, sarcasm, and some forms of humor. It also means that they sometimes need to have the impact of their behavior on others explicitly explained to them. Even if it seems obvious to others, they may not understand it. For example, a person with HFASD may not realize that she is annoying others by constantly raising her hand in class and interrupting other students to correct them.

Related Strengths

The silver lining in these difficult social deficits is independence of thinking, and the ability of people with HFASD to stay focused on what is fair, interesting, and important as opposed to getting swept away by the popularity contests and peer pressure that can lead typical teens in the wrong direction. Research has shown that while typical people will actually say that something they know to be true is false if they are in a group of people who all endorse the falsehood, people with HFASD will not. This independent thinking can lead people with HFASD to make important discoveries and stand by their principles when others give in to societal expectations. Given proper supports and teaching, people with HFASD can develop into loyal friends who value people for what they are, and are not afraid to be different in a myriad of interesting ways. John Elder Robison's 2012 book *Be Different* is an excellent guide to developing into a successful, happy person with HFASD.

Inflexible, Repetitive Thoughts and Behaviors

Rigidity

Children with HFASD are typically inflexible. Changes in routine and unexpected events are challenging, and it is easy for them to get stuck on specific ideas or behaviors. Once stuck, they get distracted from whatever task is required of them at that time (e.g., homework, getting ready in the morning, etc.). Just like the social learning problems described above, this rigidity is biologically programmed in the brain. It appears as difficulties with making transitions, negotiating, tolerating change, changing behavior in response to feedback, adjusting to the unexpected, generating new ways to approach problems, accepting different interpretations of rules, getting over strong feelings, or compromising.

Another form of rigidity is moralism, a kind of inflexible adherence to nonnegotiable moral principles that is often out of context with practical reality. An example might be a child who criticizes a parent who has run a yellow traffic light when the parent is on the way to the emergency room for treatment of a severe cut or burn. Rigidity is also found in inflexibility over matters that are of little consequence, such as arguing about whether the route to the emergency room was the quickest when it might be the difference between a few hundred yards by choosing to take one turn over another. In the classroom, this may be found when a student fixates on a perception that a teacher has not enforced a rule consistently. Such fixations on moral correctness can escalate and interfere with availability for instruction. It is important to remember at such times that many students with HFASD are rule bound and do not realize that their behavior appears disrespectful or rude.

Insistence on Sameness

Insistence on sameness is very common in HFASD. It refers to the need for things to stay the same. A child with HFASD may be deeply disturbed by a seemingly minor change in the arrangement of furniture in her living room or in the order of her bedtime routine. Any novel or unexpected situation can produce anxiety for people with HFASD. This can result in behavior that may be viewed as oppositional and can lead to meltdowns. This general rigidity is what parents, neighbors, and teachers often label as stubbornness. Children with HFASD may have many fears in addition to those related to unexpected changes in schedules. Unpredictable situations, school hallways, cafeterias, playgrounds, or bus rides can tend to overwhelm kids with HFASD. They may also be overwhelmed by unexpected academic challenges or by having too many things to remember or too many tasks to perform. They often have limited frustration tolerance and may display tantrums when thwarted. Routines and rules are very important to children with HFASD in providing a sense of needed order and structure, and hence, predictability about the world. More will be discussed about the need to ease children with HFASD into changes in school or class routines in Chapter 6.

Perseveration

Children with HFASD tend to repeat behaviors, an action referred to as stereotypic behaviors or perseveration. The child with HFASD may stare at objects or repeat behaviors that seem to have no purpose for hours at a time. This can be seen in the "flapping" of hands, pacing, or other circumscribed, repeated movements, even those that are self-injurious or destructive to others or property. Perseveration can also occur in thinking, such as in obsessive interests or the need to talk about specific things over and over. This is exemplified by fascination with a particular narrow field such as sharks, weather, train schedules, airport architecture, maps, and so on. The pursuit of a limited area of knowledge may encompass a huge amount of detail on the subject and can interfere significantly with social interactions and other important daily functions (Russell & Sofronoff, 2005).

Use of Memory in Systemizing

The term *systemizing* applies to the fascination with data that has inherent networks, such as maps, weather patterns, or subway systems. Baron-Cohen, O'Riordan, Stone, Jones, and Plaisted (1999) postulated that children with HFASD are more interested in systems that can be described as "folk physics" (an interest in how things work) versus "folk psychology" (an interest in how people work). We have found, however, that in girls with HFASD, obsessions can include human material, such as Hollywood celebrity facts. And those obsessed with World

War II and other military buffs with HFASD sometimes focus on famous military decisions by war commanders. In any case, the knowledge collected by students with HFASD is generally focused on crystallized facts instead of interpersonal processes.

Related Strengths

There are also strengths inherent in the inflexibility that characterizes HFASD. Special interests can be seen as strengths that can be utilized in the educational process to increase motivation for all kinds of learning. For example, if a student with HFASD has to work on writing skills, then it can be helpful to allow him to write about his special interest. A visual behavior reinforcement chart may be extra reinforcing if it is decorated with images of the child's special interest. As people with HFASD grow up, a special interest can evolve into an area of expertise and professional accomplishment. For example, a child who loves dinosaurs could grow up to be a paleontologist, or a child who loves computers could grow up to be a programmer. In the broadest sense, the flip side of inflexibility is perseverance and the ability to stick with something until you become an expert. The trick is to build on interests that are productive, use them to motivate learning and behavior that is otherwise hard for the child, and also help the child to control repetitive behaviors that cause problems. For example, a child who is teased or ostracized at school for pacing can work on only pacing at home in his or her own room. More generally, children with HFASD can be taught to harness their focused interests, handle the unexpected, and avoid getting stuck if these skills are explicitly taught and modeled at home. The book *Unstuck and On Target Everywhere: Teaching Executive Functions in Everyday Life* (Kenworthy et al., 2014) gives specific suggestions about how to teach flexibility when it is needed and respect inflexibility when it is not interfering.

Problems With Planning and Organization

The DSM-5 (APA, 2013), the new handbook for diagnosing HFASD as well as all other psychiatric and developmental disorders, emphasizes that executive functions are disrupted in developmental disorders such as HFASD. Executive functions are brain-based abilities that help children control their behavior (e.g., stay in their seat at school, don't interrupt) and reach their goals (e.g., finish something with multiple steps, like getting ready for school). There are many different brain-based abilities that make up executive functions, including:

» initiation (getting started);
» inhibition (impulse control, "putting on the brakes," and "thinking before acting");
» flexibility;
» working memory (keeping information in mind while performing a task);
» organization (keeping track of materials, understanding what the main point is, seeing the big picture, and knowing what the top priority is);
» planning (developing, carrying out, and modifying a plan of action such as for a science fair project); and
» self-monitoring (checking work for accuracy and keeping track of how one's behaviors affect others).

In HFASD, flexibility is a major problem, as described in the previous section, but other executive functions such as self-monitoring, planning, and organization are also affected (Kenworthy, Yerys, Anthony, & Wallace, 2008). Planning and organization are specifically identified as impaired in people with ASD in the DSM-5. The expression "can't see the forest for the trees" captures the organization style of many children with HFASD. They tend to have trouble organizing things, such as their rooms, school materials, homework, and belongings. They also have trouble identifying the main idea and organizing their thinking in ways that are accessible to most others. This means that they have trouble "showing" what they know in school, especially through writing. They struggle to get their ideas across to others, to pull information together, and to synthesize complex and different information into a cohesive whole. Reading comprehension, note-taking, studying for tests, and managing homework and long-term assignments are other academic skills that depend on good organization and integration of information and can be hard for people with HFASD. The later part of elementary school and middle school can be especially hard for children with HFASD because these academic skills become important then.

Related Strengths

This cognitive style can also be an asset. Children with HFASD tend to have an exquisite ability to memorize the smallest facts and excel at remembering details. Their heightened awareness and attention to detail may be useful in detective work (it is no accident that Sherlock Holmes shows lots of signs of HFASD), computer programming, math, engineering, medical pathology, and other jobs that require logical and detail-oriented approaches. However, they often have difficulty organizing tasks that have several steps, and setting or keeping track of goals and instructions that should guide their work. When inflexibility and a strong focus on detail combine, people with HFASD can, like Stanley in the introduction, get stuck and "nitpick" over the smallest details.

Sensory and Motor Development

Sensory difficulties are another aspect of ASD that is highlighted in the DSM-5, which has added a new ASD diagnostic symptom: "Hyper- or hyporeactivity to sensory input or unusual interest in sensory aspects of the environment (e.g., apparent indifference to pain/temperature, adverse response to specific sounds or textures, excessive smelling or touching of objects, visual fascination with lights or movement)" (APA, 2013, p. 50). Many children with HFASD show an exaggerated response to loud noises such as thunder or applause or unexpected sounds. Children with HFASD also may display tactile defensiveness; in other words, they may avoid touch, warmth, and hugs. Others seek deep pressure. Some even run into walls or people on purpose. Labels in clothes, fluorescent lights, and other irritants that seem minor can actually create major difficulty for children with HFASD and lead to irritable, anxious, or unfocused behavior. Some children with HFASDs may demonstrate simultaneous hyposensitivities and hypersensitivities. For example, they might be overly sensitive to some noises but not responsive to the human voice.

Motor clumsiness is often significant. Relatively few highly athletic children are found in the HFASD population. They may display some exquisitely developed skills such as mastery of a musical instrument, but struggle with gross motor skills like riding a bike or catching a ball. They are often awkward in tasks requiring balance and coordination. People with HFASD can be hypotonic, or show a generalized muscular weakness that affects posture, movement, strength, and coordination. Fine motor deficits make it hard for many children with HFASD to button buttons, tie shoes, and write with a pencil (MacNeil & Mostofsky, 2012). For these reasons, occupational and physical therapies are among the very earliest interventions that are employed along with speech/language therapy. Computers can be essential tools for limiting the motor demands of writing.

Language Development

Basic structural language abilities, like vocabulary and grammar, are usually good in children with HFASD, while higher order organization and pragmatic language abilities are usually impaired (Loukusa & Moilanen, 2009). Many children with HFASD have big vocabularies, and they can be precocious regarding learning the alphabet, naming colors, and counting. They may be slower, however, to put words together into meaningful sentences, and rely more on scripted language, which is copied directly from phrases they have heard on a TV show or said by another person. Most importantly, they may be less likely to use language to communicate socially or emotionally with another person. Even as infants, they may babble less than others and seem less interested in communicating through sounds or physical gestures. Their pattern of strengths and weaknesses can be very confusing to others. For example, a child may be quite verbal about a certain topic of interest, but unable to express simple feelings. Often children with HFASD struggle to internalize language or keep track of and use oral directions to guide their behavior (Wallace, Silvers, Martin, & Kenworthy, 2009).

As children with HFASD approach school age, their language is often fluent, but not always meaningful. Sentences, while formulated correctly according to grammatical rules, seem to lack functional effectiveness, or what speech and language pathologists call "communicative intent." Sometimes children with HFASD talk without attending to whether they are making any sense to the person they are talking to. This can be a reflection of the organization problems described above, when they fail to communicate the main idea or the pivotal point. It can also reflect problems with abstraction, inference, or practical, functional language. Their flexibility with word meanings can be limited, which frequently shows up in tests and instructional measures of listening comprehension. A major reason people with HFASD are referred to as "little professors" is their stiff, pedantic, and monotonic use of language. Their varied, expressive qualities of language may be unusual. This is called *prosody*, which is the pitch, loudness, tempo, stress emphasis, tonality, and rhythm patterns of spoken language.

Behavior Problems

Although behavior problems are not unusual at home or school, they are not always a major presenting problem in HFASD. Negative behavioral outbursts are most frequently related to teasing, frustration, being thwarted, or difficulties in compliance when a particularly rigid response pattern has been challenged or interrupted. Resistant, noncooperative behavior is sometimes found when areas of rigidity are challenged. Rebecca Moyes (2002), a parent of a child with HFASD, has presented a viewpoint on the development of behavior management plans for children with HFASD. She stressed the importance of first attempting to analyze the communicative intent of the negative behavior. A harsh, punitive approach to negative behavior is especially ill advised when the negative behavior was intended to communicate the child's feelings.

A feeling of being overloaded or overwhelmed can be a major source of behavior problems, whether those are outbursts or highly anxious behaviors. The typical cognitive profile in HFASD involves strengths in picking up on details and learning discrete facts and words, but difficulty integrating information and a tendency to get stuck on bits of information that might not be important. That thinking style leads easily to the individual becoming overwhelmed, especially if a situation is complicated, unfamiliar, or unexpected. The person with HFASD may take in lots of details, and yet sense that she doesn't really understand what is going on, but not know how to step back and figure it out. Then her anxiety increases, as is natural (think of being in a foreign city, where you don't speak the language and you realize you are lost), and then various negative behaviors can emerge. Some children with HFASD get more impulsive and can say or do mean things, others get more repetitive and stuck, and still others withdraw into a nonresponsive state. If a child with HFASD is showing lots of negative behaviors, then it is important to consider whether or not she is overloaded. Most of us cannot improve our behavior or learn new ways of responding when we are overwhelmed.

School Concerns

Just as parents have difficulties in identifying the early signs of HFASD, teachers also may be uncertain of key features to address educationally. During the individual development of the child, parents and teachers must take notice as skills blossom or fail to develop as expected. Many children suspected of HFASD are brought to the psychiatry, psychology, or early childhood departments of pediatric medical centers. Other children with HFASD in the U.S. are spotted as having unique delays by child find screenings and soon receive pull-out or part-time programs for preschool children with developmental delays. They may require speech/language, occupational, and physical therapy interventions. They are monitored for further crystallization of symptoms. Frequently, behavior management programs and parent support programs are employed.

There are many school jurisdictions, however, where these early assessment and intervention opportunities are not in place. Early on, children suspected of delays might be classified generally as having developmental delays, an umbrella category. They may be seen as multiply handicapped or multiply disabled. They may be placed in a diagnostic center or in a diagnostic mode while they are being monitored. Schools are some of the best laboratories for differentiating appropriate classification schemes, as the strengths and weaknesses crystallize in the child's attempts to absorb, adapt to, and master the world of learning. The problems children with ASD face in school will be covered in greater detail in Chapters 5 and 6. Tips for helping your child succeed in school are included in Chapters 5, 6, and 7.

Community Concerns

Many parents worry about their child's ability to function in the community related to limitations in adaptive behavior. Adaptive behavior encompasses those behaviors critical to living independently, including daily living skills (e.g., dressing and grooming oneself, grocery shopping, using public transportation, crossing the street safely, making purchases, etc.), social skills, and communication skills (e.g., using the words of others to guide one's own behavior, expressing oneself clearly, knowing how and when to ask for help, picking up on a cues that another person is getting frustrated in a conversation). Children with ASD typically have adaptive behavior impairments across all areas. In addition to deficits in communication and socialization, they display poorer daily living skills than their typically developing peers and children with other developmental disorders (Gillham, Carter, Volkmar, & Sparrow, 2000; Klin et al., 2007). Even very bright children with HFASD show big gaps in their adaptive skills (Kenworthy et al., 2005; Kenworthy, Case, Harms, Martin, & Wallace, 2009). As a result, many parents fear for their child's safety, wondering if he would know how to communicate effectively if stopped by a policeman, for example. Other parents wonder if their child will ever gain the skills to leave home when she grows up because she struggles so much with basic hygiene, food preparation, laundry skills, etc. Perhaps most profoundly, parents worry that their child will not have the social skills to develop meaningful relationships outside of their family of origin. They wonder who will look out for their child when they themselves pass on.

Because these are all painful thoughts, and also because adaptive deficits are not always obvious at school, adaptive skill deficits often get ignored in childhood. Especially with bright children, a pattern can develop in which parents are compensating for, or ignoring, the most basic adaptive skill deficits even as their son or daughter moves into adolescence. This not only puts children at risk for difficulty living independently as adults, it also puts children at immediate risk for being bullied or teased (a middle schooler with bad body odor is an immediate target), isolated from peers (a high schooler who does not know how to use public transportation cannot participate in some group activities), and misunderstood by teachers (a student who lacks the communication skills to ask for clarification when confused is easily mistaken for a lazy person who does not care). Evaluating and teaching basic adaptive skills from an early age is essential if children with HFASD are to be happy, well-functioning members of their community.

chapter 3

Recognizing and Diagnosing HFASD

Concerned about her lack of progress both at home and in preschool, Celia's parents finally came to agreement that they needed to find out what might be the cause of her problems. A close friend recommended a pediatrician, who focused on her inattentiveness and diagnosed Attention Deficit/Hyperactivity Disorder (ADHD). Celia's mother had a gut feeling that there must be something more. ADHD didn't explain Celia's lack of social connection, her focus on certain topics, or her difficult behavior when asked to transition to new activities or participate in a group. Celia's teacher suggested that her parents have her evaluated by a behavioral specialist, who suggested Oppositional Defiant Disorder, which again didn't seem to completely explain the causes or solutions to Celia's unique set of challenges. As she entered kindergarten and then first grade, the discrepancy between how obviously bright she was and how strong her reading was versus her poor performance in writing and math led Celia's parents to request a psychoeducational evaluation, which suggested probable learning disabilities. It was not until third grade that a knowledgeable teacher and school psychologist took a fresh look at Celia's case. Subsequently, HFASD was accurately diagnosed as the source of Celia's struggles. This opened the door to a better understanding of Celia's strengths and needs and led to getting appropriate services in the school and in the community.

The diagnosis of HFASD is considerably challenging for many professionals. It certainly can be difficult for parents who are concerned about their children. Many parents naturally turn to the Internet or friends to find available guidelines for diagnostic classifications. Parents' observations and intimate knowledge of their child's development are important sources in working with professionals to arrive at an accurate diagnosis. In this chapter, we hope to explain how professionals, parents, and other stakeholders are becoming more precise in determining diagnosis. Only a trained mental health professional is qualified to make an accurate diagnosis. Please do not attempt to diagnose your child on your own or trust in the accuracy and reliability of Internet-based tests and checklists.

Myths About HFASD

The following are unproven myths about the identification of HFASD:

- All persons with HFASD can be identified by their stronger verbal than performance IQs.
- All persons with HFASD have above-average intelligence.
- People with HFASD all want to communicate with others but don't know how.

- People with HFASD don't want to communicate with others.
- All "nerdy" people have a touch of HFASD.
- Autism is a perfect spectrum or continuity of symptom intensity and frequency.
- A high number of autistic symptoms rules out functional capacity in persons with HFASD or other forms of autism.

Why Is Early Identification Important?

Charman, Howlin, Berry, and Prince (2004) conducted a study that included the diagnostic experiences of parents of children with autism and parents of children identified with HFASD. Results demonstrated that parents of children diagnosed as having autism typically became aware of problems in the child's development at an earlier age than parents of children with HFASD. They sought help earlier and received a diagnosis much sooner. The average age of the child when he or she was diagnosed with HFASD was 11.13 years compared to 5.49 years for autism. Although the average age of diagnosis of HFASD has dropped recently to 6 years, 3 months (CDC, 2012), it remains the case that many children do not receive a clear diagnosis of HFASD until they are of school age (McConachie, Le Couteur, & Honey, 2005).

Critical research is now ongoing in efforts to make the accurate diagnosis of HFASD as early as possible. It has been clearly demonstrated with other forms of autism that early, intensive intervention makes a great difference in the future of the child with autism. It is extremely important, then, that HFASD be identified early in order to protect and enrich the quality of life of these children.

Why Is Accurate Diagnosis Important?

What we know of adults living with the disorder without benefit of accurate diagnosis early in life is that they suffer in independent living, their social life, and the world of work. Frequently, significant emotional problems and even mental illness may result from this developmental disability. Fortunately, diagnosis and intervention at any age can be helpful.

HFASD is a biologically based, unique way of seeing, interpreting, coping with, and acting in the world. Because HFASD is hard-wired, the diagnosis helps to direct parents and teachers to lifelong interventions appropriate to the condition, as well as alerting them to strengths that can be built on as children with HFASD grow. Failure to identify it, and to do so early, may doom parents and teachers to set goals and expectations that are unrealistic and disappointing. If HFASD is not identified, then mental health professionals can misdiagnose the person as having something else. In the past, people with HFASD have been thought to be paranoid, because they sometimes became increasingly defensive as their attempts to relate to others failed through misinterpretation of others' behaviors and motives. They lost trust in others as they lost trust in themselves and in their ability to effectively interpret, and hence, manipulate the social environment. Other misdiagnoses that can occur if HFASD is not identified are schizophrenia, Obsessive-Compulsive Disorder, and Oppositional Defiant Disorder.

How Is the Diagnosis of HFASD Made?

Mental health professionals such as psychiatrists, clinical psychologists, school psychologists, licensed professional counselors, and social workers often are the first to make the diagnosis of ASD, and they need clear guidelines to help them make this identification. Definitive diagnosis of ASD is best made by a team of child specialists with specific training and experience with ASD. Diagnosis of ASD requires a detailed interview with a parent regarding early developmental history and current functioning, and an interview with the child, often conducted in the form of a play interview if the child is elementary school age or younger. Because the diagnosis cannot be made based on a simple test, but requires the integration of information regarding lots of different behaviors, specialized training and experience is needed.

Prior to a formal diagnostic evaluation, screening tools can be used to assess the likelihood that a person might have an ASD and identify people who should receive comprehensive assessments. Commonly used rating scales include the Social Communication Questionnaire (SCQ), the Autism Quotient (AQ), and the Social Responsiveness Scale-2 (SRS). Parents and adults with HFASD are cautioned against taking rating scale tests on the Internet as a substitute for consulting with an experienced clinician.

What are the specific behaviors required to make the ASD diagnosis? Let's take a detailed look at the newest diagnostic guidelines, from the DSM-5 (APA, 2013). ASD is diagnosed by the presence of the following behavioral characteristics:

A. Persistent deficits in social communication and social interaction across multiple contexts, as manifested by the following, currently or by history:
Deficits in social-emotional reciprocity, ranging for example, from abnormal social approach and failure of normal back-and-forth conversation to reduced sharing of interests, emotions, or affect; to failure to initiate or respond to social interactions.
Deficits in nonverbal communicative behaviors used for social interaction, ranging for example, from poorly integrated verbal and nonverbal communication; to abnormalities in eye contact and body language or defi-

cits in understanding and use of gestures; to total lack of facial expression and nonverbal communication.

Deficits in developing, maintaining, and understanding relationships, ranging, for example from difficulties adjusting behavior to suit various social contexts; to difficulties sharing imaginative play or in making friends; to absence of interest in peers.

B. Restricted, repetitive patterns of behavior, interests, or activities, as manifested by at least two of the following, currently or by history:

Stereotyped or repetitive motor movements, use of objects, or speech (e.g. simple motor stereotypies, lining up toys or flipping objects, echolalia, idiosyncratic phrases).

Insistence on sameness, inflexible adherence to routines, or ritualized patterns of verbal or nonverbal behavior (e.g. extreme distress at small changes, difficulties with transitions, rigid thinking patterns, greeting rituals, need to take same route or eat same food every day).

Highly restricted, fixated interests that are abnormal in intensity or focus (e.g. strong attachment to or preoccupation with unusual objects, excessively circumscribed or perseverative interests).

Hyper- or hyporeactivity to sensory input or unusual interest in sensory aspects of the environment (e.g. apparent indifference to pain/temperature, adverse reactions to specific sounds or textures, excessive smelling or touching of objects, visual fascination with lights or movement).

C. Symptoms must be present in the early developmental period (but may not become fully manifest until social demands exceed limited capacities, or may be masked by learned strategies in later life).

D. Symptoms cause clinically significant impairment in social, occupational, or other important areas of current functioning. (p. 50)

A diagnosis of ASD is made when a clinician finds that a child has sufficient problems in both category A (social interaction and communication) and category B (restricted and repetitive interests and behaviors), and that the problems were present when the child was young and are currently impairing his or her functioning. In addition to the diagnosis, the clinician indicates whether there is "accompanying intellectual or language impairment." On the face of it, the child with HFASD would appear to be a person who meets the criteria above without also having accompanying intellectual or language impairment. It is likely that many children who previously received an Asperger's diagnosis will now be characterized in this way.

Differential Diagnosis: What Other Diagnoses Are Confused With HFASD?

The process of identifying a person as belonging to one diagnostic category as opposed to another with similar characteristics is called *differential diagnosis*. There are a number of conditions that overlap with HFASD. Some of them are Social Communication Disorder, social anxiety, hyperlexia, and nonverbal learning disabilities.

Social Communication Disorder (SCD) is a new diagnosis that is meant for people who struggle with similar social communication skills to those that are impaired in ASD, but do not have impairing repetitive behaviors or rigidity. Referring to DSM-5 diagnostic criteria for ASD listed earlier in this chapter, the symptoms under category A, "Persistent deficits in social communication and social interaction," are similar symptoms as seen in SCD, but the symptoms listed under category B,

"Restricted, repetitive patterns of behavior, interests, or activities," are not seen in SCD. It is important to understand that if a child has a current impairing condition with social deficits and either had restricted behaviors in the past or currently has them, the diagnosis of ASD is more appropriate than SCD.

Social anxiety is a specific anxiety, as opposed to a full-time anxious state, which relates primarily to apprehension about initiating social relationships or contact. A key difference between social anxiety and HFASD is that a person with HFASD has cognitive trouble understanding social cues, regardless of whether or not she is feeling anxious, while the socially anxious person understands social information but has trouble in social situations because his anxiety interferes with his ability to communicate effectively.

Hyperlexia is a condition that some persons with HFASD have. It is a language disorder characterized by early precocious reading and/or intense fascination with letters and numbers. This is accompanied by limited comprehension of what is read, difficulty with verbal language, difficulties with social interaction, and other autistic traits.

Nonverbal Learning Disability (NLD) is not a DSM-5 diagnosis, but it is a term that is applied to children who have good reading decoding and rote learning skills, but problems with social skills, pragmatic language, anxiety, math, visual problem solving, organization, and motor skills. There are obvious overlaps between HFASD and NLD, including problems with social skills, pragmatic language, and motor and organization skills (Rourke & Tsatsanis, 2000; Volkmar & Klin, 1998). A major difference is that the criteria for an NLD do not include the repetitive, restricted behavior symptoms seen in HFASD, and HFASD criteria do not include good rote learning and decoding, but problems with math and visual problem solving. It is possible to meet criteria for both HFASD and NLD, but those children with NLD without repetitive restrictive behaviors would likely be given a DSM-5 diagnosis of SCD (see above) and Specific Learning Disorder, not HFASD.

From reading the above descriptions, it is evident that distinguishing HFASD from many similar conditions is a challenge not only for parents but also for clinicians. In addition to teasing apart symptoms in order to best understand the appropriate diagnosis, a good assessment should also provide a detailed profile of the individual's cognitive and language abilities. Diagnosis and an understanding of cognitive strengths and weaknesses are both needed to develop effective educational and treatment plans. This comprehensive understanding is required in order to not only understand how to accommodate and teach to a person's weaknesses, but also how to build on her strengths.

Neurological "Soft Signs"

The following are features shared by many (but not all) neurodevelopmental disabilities and often found in HFASD. They do not necessarily act as pivotal features in making diagnoses, but they are important in recognizing that characteristics overlap between disorders. Because they offer important hints, these features are called soft signs, and must be addressed educationally. Often, these features are not addressed and prove to be frustrating to teachers. Parents are already familiar with these features from child rearing, but they don't always appear in specialist reports because testing is often done in one-on-one conditions. They also often are not addressed in Individualized Education Programs (IEPs) or other school intervention plans, such as Section 504 plans. However, when they are addressed in IEPs and 504 plans they can make a world of difference in the way achievement targets can be met. These features include:

- » irritability;
- » motor automatisms like tics and tremors;
- » low frustration tolerance;

» fatigue;
» lack of perseverance;
» lack of resilience;
» stubbornness;
» oppositionality;
» emotional immaturity;
» emotional vulnerability;
» emotional lability (unpredictable propensity to change);
» impulsivity;
» explosiveness;
» auditory or visual perceptual discrimination errors;
» problems with articulation and slow and uneven pacing of words, and retrieval, hesitation, or immaturity in formulation;
» somatic complaints including headaches;
» gross and fine-motor awkwardness, poor coordination, or balance;
» sequential, short-term, and working memory problems;
» impaired comprehension;
» limitations in judgment; and
» general problems in executive functioning.

The above characteristics in themselves are not diagnostic of any single disability and may not always be always present in HFASD or any of its possible coexisting conditions; however, they can be flags or markers to alert us to some of the barriers to classroom instruction.

Diagnosing ASD in a High-Functioning Adult

Little research has been conducted on existing normed personality tests for the use of identification of ASD in adults. Because ASD involves some commonly shared personality characteristics, there is hope that in the future there will be better accuracy in diagnosing ASD when suspected in adulthood. The gold standard clinical interview for people with ASD, the Autism Diagnostic Observation Schedule-2, has an adult module that is useful when administered by a trained clinician, but early childhood history can be hard to obtain if the adult's parents are not available. Some of the work of Ozonoff, Garcia, Clark, and Lainhart (2005) is promising in using such instruments as the Minnesota Multiphasic Personality Inventory-2 (MMPI-2), which reveals some consistency in response patterns with adults.

The following are some characteristics from a list prepared by Roger N. Meyer, an adult who reported about his own experiences as a person with Asperger's Syndrome, and Tony Attwood. Meyer and Attwood (2001) noted that these characteristics are distinguished in adults with HFASD because of their consistency of appearance, intensity, and the high number of them that appear simultaneously. However, they also wrote that not every one of these characteristics will apply to adults with ASD.

Social Characteristics

- » Difficulty in accepting criticism or correction.
- » Difficulty in offering correction or criticism without appearing harsh, pedantic or insensitive.
- » Difficulty in perceiving and applying unwritten social rules or protocols.
- » "Immature" manners.
- » Failure to distinguish between private and public personal care habits (i.e., brushing, public attention to skin problems, nose picking, teeth picking, ear canal cleaning, clothing arrangement).
- » Naive trust in others.
- » Shyness.
- » Low or no conversational participation in group meetings or conferences.

» Constant anxiety about performance and acceptance, despite recognition and commendation.

» Scrupulous honesty, often expressed in an apparently disarming or inappropriate manner or setting.

» Bluntness in emotional expression.

» "Flat affect."

» Discomfort manipulating or "playing games" with others.

» Unmodulated reaction in being manipulated, patronized, or "handled" by others.

» Low to medium level of paranoia.

» Low to no apparent sense of humor; bizarre sense of humor (often stemming from a "private" internal thread of humor being inserted in public conversation without preparation or warming others up to the reason for the "punch line").

» Difficulty with reciprocal displays of pleasantries and greetings.

» Problems expressing empathy or comfort to/with others: sadness, condolence, congratulations, etc.

» Pouting, ruminating, fixating on bad experiences with people or events for an inordinate length of time.

» Difficulty with adopting a social mask to obscure real feelings, moods, reactions.

» Using social masks inappropriately.

» Abrupt and strong expression of likes and dislikes.

» Rigid adherence to rules and social conventions where flexibility is desirable.

» Apparent absence of relaxation, recreational, or "time out" activities.

» "Serious" all the time.

» Known for single-mindedness.

» Flash temper.

» Tantrums.

» Excessive talk.

» Difficulty in forming friendships and intimate relationships; difficulty in distinguishing between acquaintance and friendship.

» Social isolation and intense concern for privacy.

» Limited clothing preference; discomfort with formal attire or uniforms.

» Preference for bland or bare environments in living arrangements.

» Difficulty judging others' personal space.

» Limited by intensely pursued interests.

» Often perceived as "being in their own world."

Physical Manifestations

» Strong sensory sensitivities: touch and tactile sensations, sounds, lighting and colors, odors, taste.

» Clumsiness.

» Balance difficulties.

» Difficulty in judging distances, height, depth.

» Difficulty in recognizing others' faces (prosopagnosia).

» Stims (self-stimulatory behavior serving to reduce anxiety, stress, or to express pleasure).

» Self-injurious or disfiguring behaviors.

» Nail-biting.

» Unusual gait, stance, posture.

» Gross or fine motor coordination problems.

» Low apparent sexual interest.

» Depression.

» Anxiety.

» Sleep difficulties.

» Verbosity.

» Difficulty expressing anger (excessive or "bottled up").

» Flat or monotone vocal expression; limited range of inflection.

» Difficulty with initiating or maintaining eye contact.

» Elevated voice volume during periods of stress and frustration.

» Strong food preferences and aversions.

» Unusual and rigidly adhered to eating behaviors.

» Bad or unusual personal hygiene.

Cognitive Characteristics

» Susceptibility to distraction.

» Difficulty in expressing emotions.

» Resistance to or failure to respond to talk therapy.

» Mental shutdown response to conflicting demands and multi-tasking.

» Generalized confusion during periods of stress.

» Low understanding of the reciprocal rules of conversation: interrupting, dominating, minimum participation, difficult in shifting topics, problem with initiating or terminating conversation, subject perseveration.

» Insensitivity to the non-verbal cues of others (stance, posture, facial expressions).

» Perseveration best characterized by the term "bulldog tenacity."

» Literal interpretation of instructions (failure to read between the lines).

» Interpreting words and phrases literally (problem with colloquialisms, clichés, neologism, turns of phrase, common humorous expressions).

» Preference for visually oriented instruction and training.

» Dependence on step-by-step learning procedures (disorientation occurs when a step is assumed, deleted, or otherwise overlooked in instruction).

» Difficulty in generalizing.

» Preference for repetitive, often simple routines.

» Difficulty in understanding rules for games of social entertainment.

» Missing or misconstruing others' agendas, priorities, preferences.

» Impulsiveness.

» Compelling need to finish one task completely before starting another.

» Rigid adherence to rules and routines.

» Difficulty in interpreting meaning to others' activities; difficulty in drawing relationships between an activity or event and ideas.

» Exquisite attention to detail, principally visual, or details that can be visualized ("Thinking in Pictures") or cognitive details (often those learned by rote).

» Concrete thinking.

» Distractibility due to focus on external or internal sensations, thoughts, and/or sensory input (appearing to be in a world of one's own or day-dreaming).

» Difficulty in assessing relative importance of details (an aspect of the trees/forest problem).

» Poor judgment of when a task is finished (often attributable to perfectionism or an apparent unwillingness to follow differential standards for quality).

» Difficulty in imagining others' thoughts in a similar or identical event or circumstance that are different from one's own ("Theory of Mind" issues).

» Difficulty with organizing and sequencing (planning and execution; successful performance of tasks in a logical, functional order).

» Difficulty in assessing cause and effect relationships (behaviors and consequences).

» An apparent lack of "common sense."

» Relaxation techniques and developing recreational "release" interest may require formal instruction.

» Rage, tantrum, shutdown, self-isolating reactions appearing "out of nowhere."

» Substantial hidden self-anger, anger towards others, and resentment.

» Difficulty in estimating time to complete tasks.

» Difficulty in learning self-monitoring techniques.

» Disinclination to produce expected results in an orthodox manner.

» Psychometric testing shows great deviance between verbal and performance results.

» Extreme reaction to changes in routine, surroundings, and people.

» Stilted, pedantic conversational style ("The Professor").

Note. From *Asperger's Syndrome Employment Workbook: An Employment Workbook for Adults With Asperger's Syndrome* (p. 306), by R. N. Meyer and T. Attwood, 2001, Philadelphia, PA: Jessica Kingsley. Copyright © 2001 Jessica Kingsley. Reprinted by permission of Jessica Kingsley Publishers.

After Diagnosis with HFASD: Evaluate Cognitive, Language, and Motor Abilities

If a person receives an HFASD diagnosis without also getting cognitive, educational, language, and motor assessments, then each of these should be considered because they can add important information about what weaknesses need to be accommodated and targeted in therapies, and what strengths can be built upon. These evaluations can also be essential for getting public school special education services and building an effective school plan. A diagnosis doesn't capture the unique abilities and disabilities of a person. As we noted earlier, Stephen Shore's comment, "If you've met one person with autism, you've met one person with autism," expresses a profound truth about how different people with HFASD can be from each other. It is also true that people with HFASD are more likely than people with other disabilities to have peaks and valleys in their cognitive, language, and motor abilities. Whereas a person with intellectual disability often has a relatively flat profile, many people with HFASD have remarkable strengths as well as major weaknesses.

Understanding the person's communication and motor skills is essential to early treatment planning, and often young children are assessed by a team of psychology, speech-language, and occupational therapy specialists who can describe functioning across cognitive, communication, and motor domains and make recommendations for treatment. Communication is a fundamental gateway skill to all kinds of learning. A speech and language therapist is essential for unlocking the complicated pattern of strengths and weaknesses typically seen in the language of children with HFASD (see previous chapter). It is usually helpful for the child with HFASD to receive periodic speech and language assessments throughout her development to identify progress and new targets for intervention to improve communication skills. It is essential that the assessments not just focus on the core structural language skills (e.g., vocabulary, grammar, phonology) that are often strengths for people with HFASD, but also evaluate "higher order" language skills for formulating and organizing sentences and conversation and pragmatic language skills as well. Occupational and physical therapy assessments can identify motor impediments to writing, sitting still in class, and other key school-related skills and suggest ways to accommodate motor weaknesses (e.g., write on a computer) and also therapies to strengthen motor skills.

It is also essential to understand the cognitive profile of children with HFASD. The combination of good vocabulary, strong verbal knowledge, strengths in perceiving visual patterns, and problems with social reasoning, organization, and flexibility tends to lead to variability on intelligence tests, with some areas of very high performance and other areas that are more impaired (Goldstein et al., 2008; Mayes & Calhoun, 2008; Oliveras-Rentas, Kenworthy, Roberson, Martin, & Wallace, 2012). Understanding which cognitive skills are strengths and which are weaknesses empowers teachers and parents to help a child leverage her abilities to compensate for areas of difficulty. A good cognitive assessment helps parents, teachers, and others working with people with HFASD, not to mention the person with HFASD herself, to better understand what is truly hard for her versus what she is choosing not to do.

Without a clear assessment, the academic and social problems of people with HFASD are often blamed on their lack of effort or sloppiness or not caring when in fact they are struggling with specific learning problems that are masked by their strengths in other areas. People with HFASD can reason, but they do not always comprehend the core, vital, or central meaning being expressed when listening to or watching someone or something. They don't always seem to identify or register what is important. And, they may lack the judgment to use information in making practical, wise decisions. Myles and Simpson

(1998) pointed out that students with HFASD frequently lack common sense and an awareness of how to apply rules of social interchange flexibly to adapt to various contexts. Their level of vocabulary and amount of pure verbosity may lead the listener to assume that they have good inferential skills, when, in fact, they are unable to make appropriate abstractions from the facts that they collect. Mottron (2004) reported that the ability to label things verbally was one of the strongest verbal skills in high-functioning persons with ASD. However, students with HFASD may demonstrate good vocabulary skills on tests and in the classroom, but their practical comprehension may not be at the same level.

What to Expect From a Psychological Assessment

There are several different kinds of psychological assessment that will help you to understand the specific types of learning and thinking that are easy and those that are harder for a person with HFASD:

» a cognitive evaluation assesses intelligence;
» a psychoeducational evaluation assesses intelligence and academic skills for reading, writing, math, etc.;
» a neuropsychological evaluation assesses brain-based strengths and weaknesses across many functional domains, including general intelligence, executive functions, language, visual spatial abilities, learning/memory, social problem solving abilities, fine motor skills (including a timed measure of handwriting skills);
» any of these evaluations can also include assessment of current emotional status.

It is always important to understand the intelligence profile of a person with HFASD. As a child reaches school age, more detailed patterns of strength and weakness within the cognitive profile are evident and a neuropsychological evaluation that delves deeply into this pattern is appropriate and helpful. We previously discussed the typical pattern of executive dysfunction in HFASD and how that interferes with cognitive abilities to flexibly integrate information, plan, and problem solve efficiently. Executive function deficits, combined with social learning and fine motor output weakness, constitute the most common pattern of cognitive weaknesses in HFASD. The pattern is best understood through a neuropsychological evaluation. Furthermore, a neuropsychological evaluation typically explores learning and memory skills and can elucidate how the person learns best (e.g., with verbal or visual information, with big or little chunks of data, with meaningful information or through rote repetition). Information on how a person learns can be invaluable for improving school progress and adjustment.

Each of these types of cognitive evaluation should also include the assessment of adaptive skills, or what skills the person with HFASD actually demonstrates at home, school, and in the community in terms of daily living, communication, and socialization. Adaptive assessments are especially important for people with HFASD, who often have a big gap between what they know (intelligence) and how they can use what they know in daily life (adaptive skills; Kenworthy et al., 2005). Other key components of any cognitive assessment include play or an interview with the child to explore his hopes, dreams, self-concept, and fears and a thorough medical, family, birth, developmental, and educational history that captures the child's strengths and weaknesses as perceived by his parents and teachers. Because learning disabilities, especially in reading comprehension and written expression (Mayes & Calhoun, 2008), are common in HFASD, some form of academic achievement assessment is also almost always needed. Finally, a good cognitive assessment of any type addresses common comorbidities, or other problems that are often seen in HFASD and can require specific treatments, including attention, anxiety, depression, impairments in self-esteem, and other behavioral psychopathologies. Just as with speech and language evaluations, it is important to periodically repeat cognitive assessments throughout a child's development to monitor progress and identify new treatment targets.

Common Pitfalls in the Assessment of People With HFASD

Although assessment of children with HFASD or any other form of autism is crucial, it also complicated. Professionals with specific experience in dealing with this population should conduct assessments of children suspected of having ASD. Scores, particularly IQ scores, must be viewed with caution. The following are among considerations to take when evaluating for HFASD:

> » Children with ASD experience irregular, incomplete, and delayed emergence of developmental systems. Many normed test instruments may assume a fixed, incremental developmental sequence, which is not present in students with ASD.

> » Autism, by definition, is almost always accompanied by deficits in the ability to have typical bonding experiences with others. Reciprocal social contact is generally a significant weakness. To be accurate, most tests require a working level of rapport that cannot always be assumed to exist in children with autism. Adapted interpersonal cueing methods are often needed, and frequently improvised, to be clear that the child registers stimulus and response demands.

> » Children with autism often have communication deficits. Test selection must be carefully attempted to circumvent or avoid these issues, because test items requiring a high level of communication will not yield valid results.

Simplified instructions are usually necessary. Items that require formulated, lengthy verbal responses frequently are not appropriate.

» Children with HFASD may display significant immaturity in the development of independent, adaptive self-care skills. This is not to be confused with the absence of adaptive skills found in those with intellectual disabilities.

» Children with HFASD have difficulties with holding verbal information in mind. Thus they struggle to keep track of directions and carry out multistep tasks (Wallace et al., 2009). They may not recognize the relevance and importance of stimuli that normally are targeted by typical children. They may perform worse on psychological tests because of their difficulty tracking and using the examiner's directions.

» Sustained effort in attending, participating, and completing assessments or assessment items may require the presence of other adults familiar to the child, such as the child's teacher or paraeducator in cases when the child's symptoms would otherwise block access to instructions and participation in general. Many tests and best practices assume that there are no helpers, including parents, involved in the one-on-one testing process.

» Sustained effort in attending, participating, and completing assessments or assessment items may require the use of systems of behavioral modification, rewards, and other reinforcements. Children with autism may require very personally engineered external incentive systems for completing tasks that most children might not require.

» Children with HFASD have difficulty making transitions from one activity to another and with comprehending and registering new rules for unfamiliar tasks. Changing from one test item's demand to another may not be smooth. It cannot be assumed that children with

HFASD are able to generalize and sustain the instructional set or demands from one subtest item to the next.

» Children with HFASD often lack frustration tolerance for extended mental effort as required by many test instruments. Testing may require more frequent breaks and more test sessions.

» Children with HFASD may not understand timed tasks and the need to hurry or be efficient. The fact that a test is timed is not always fully grasped by many students with neurological disorders. It should be determined that the student being tested fully understands the test item task requirement, or the item should not be administered. Because of the standardized nature of these tests, the instructions or expectations cannot be modified. Significant modifications to any instruction or item reduce the accuracy of the measures obtained.

» Pattern analysis of IQ tests of persons with HFASD suggests that there may also be problems with visual-motor speed, especially when using a writing implement (such as a pen or pencil). In addition, children with HFASD may have slow processing speed. All too often, processing speed is only measured on tests that require a pencil. Processing speed is a simple term that can include many parts in a mental activity and is almost never specified. For example, it may include retrieval of facts or action routines. It may include the actual internal, sequential execution of a series of steps. It may include the initiation or beginning of a task and formulation of a new strategy or other utilization of memory. Tests of visual-motor speed, especially with a pencil, are often included in IQ tests. Because motor awkwardness is a characteristic of ASD, these subtests tend to pull IQ test scores artificially downward (Kenworthy, Yerys, Weinblatt, Abrams, & Wallace, 2013). Many test developers have argued against having motor-speeded tests included as part of the IQ examination, but most popular tests still employ them. So when the term *processing speed* is referred to in a test as an index of ability, it almost always refers to a complex assortment of actions in one task that usually has a motor requirement.

» Rating scales administered to significant stakeholders in the child's life have proven to be valid and reliable, but they are subject to bias. Defensiveness, optimism, and other general impressions and expectations can color the accuracy of ratings. Hence, multiple raters should be employed. Furthermore, it is very important that ratings are administered across two or more settings, especially in the case of adaptive measures.

Many school systems use purely visual tests like the Raven's Progressive Matrices to determine giftedness. Some kids with HFASD also are gifted, but often are not identified as such. This primarily visual/spatial test places many children with HFASD at a distinct disadvantage. If some children have weaker spatial abilities and a spatial test is all that is given, then more representative ability measures are needed.

Final Note: A Good Assessment Drives Treatment

An assessment is not complete until parents (and the child, if she is an adolescent or older) have received clear, understandable feedback about what the assessment revealed (Kenworthy, 2011). At the end of the assessment process, the family should have a good understanding of how the child processes information and learns, what situations and learning demands are likely to be hard for the child, and also where the child's strengths lie. Furthermore, the assessment should result in oral feedback and a written report that clearly documents the child's diagnoses, strengths, and weaknesses, and what accommodations, teaching strategies, and therapies are indicated. Assessments should result in specific recommendations for school and other treatment that are clear and understandable to the family and to all members of the school and treatment team (Kenworthy & Anthony, 2012).

chapter 4

Developing an Intervention Plan

Katie is now a tenth grader who has been lucky to have very informed and dedicated parents. Katie was suspected of having HFASD when first tested by a psychologist specializing in autism as a 2-year-old. Through multidisciplinary assessment and monitoring, this diagnosis has been confirmed. Katie loves music, plays the piano, and sings. She has excellent language skills, but doesn't really know how to initiate and maintain friendships easily. She does pretty well communicating while shopping at the mall, or other daily activities, but she wishes she had more friends. Katie grew up being obsessed with her "Hello Kitty" scrapbook and toy collection and, at the age of 15, still continues to think a lot about her "Hannah Montana" scrapbook too.

Katie attended private schools through middle school, and is now successfully mainstreamed in a public high school with the support of a wonderful school team of dedicated professionals. She sings in the high school chorus. She has a detailed and appropriate IEP, and transition discussions are beginning. Katie has tested in the above-average range in intellectual assessments and does well in academic subjects, but her pace can be slow. She receives extra time on tests because of her slow speed in registering information and formulating appropriate written responses.

After being evaluated by an occupational therapist, Katie continued receiving occupational therapy services privately. These were dropped in ninth grade when her goals were clearly mastered. She continues to have speech/language therapy in school for pragmatic communication skills. Her speech therapist often communicates with Katie's psychotherapist about social language.

Katie has been receiving psychotherapy services since elementary school. Therapy involves a variety of approaches, including direct social skills instruction, executive skill coaching, and Cognitive Behavior Therapy for anxiety, with continued emphasis on "putting herself in other peoples' shoes." Her psychologist communicates regularly with Katie's psychiatrist, who has been prescribing and monitoring medication for anxiety for many years. Katie also attends a social skills group where she can practice some of the social language communication scripts she has studied with her speech therapist. Katie has chores at home and rehearses independence skills so that she might function on her own in a dorm room or apartment someday. She has learned the subway system. Her parents have regular meetings with her psychologist, who has been monitoring her progress since she was a toddler. The psychologist sometimes attends school IEP team meetings. Katie also enjoys participating on her IEP team and has become quite a vocal self-advocate at these meetings. With her comprehensive treatment plan in place, Katie has made continual progress and her future looks bright.

Scientific, evidence-based treatment begins with a comprehensive assessment as outlined in Chapter 3 of this book.

A comprehensive assessment may lead to an understanding of what to expect in a wide range of specific developmental and skill areas. Despite the accuracy of assessments, there are limits to how precisely the future can be predicted. For example, can anyone predict at the beginning of first grade what an eighth grader will look like prior to moving on to high school? Child development is a process, often with great variability, especially in puberty and adolescence. For the purposes of planning, however, the psychological or neuropsychological evaluation should be interpreted by the evaluator to parents with a view toward the future. Assessments are snapshots taken in moments in time, but they can help predict the situations and demands that are likely to be hardest for a child, and also those in which they are most likely to succeed.

The following are important components of the summary and recommendation sections of an autism assessment. Many of the key interventions for HFASD occur in the school setting, so a primary component of the treatment plan and recommendations in a comprehensive assessment apply there.

» A summary should include a diagnostic statement of prioritized disability areas/challenges. There are only 14 federally recognized disability areas for special education eligibility. The appropriate areas should be suggested, even though it is the school system's IEP team that assigns the disability classification for special education purposes.

» Suggested intervals for monitoring progress if some of the diagnoses require conditions to be ruled out or in, or to determine if recommendations are being effected. An IEP team can stipulate a review period in 30, 45, 60, 90, or any number of days. It is not necessary to wait for an annual review to see if recommendations are working.

» What are the educational environment placement needs for the child? This will include teacher/pupil ratio and other characteristics. Is placement in a small separate class within a school, a separate program, or separate facility required? Are there medical conditions that require a school nurse in the building and not just a health technician? For example, some students with autism have seizures or need multiple medications throughout the day. Will the school program require the presence of a full-time counselor for social/emotional/behavioral emergencies? Will the student require a part-time or full-time aide ("shadow")? Will the school require behavioral support or other consultations?

» Does the student require that some or all academic subjects be taught by a special educator?

» Does the school team need to include people who are trained in and experienced with working with students with HFASD?

» What related services will be required? These may include speech/language services, occupational therapy, or physical therapy, among other services.

» Does the student require a Behavior Intervention Plan?

» What accommodations are required for teaching and for testing?

» Is assistive technology required (such as a laptop or text-to-speech technology, tablet, etc.)?

» Will extended school year services need to be considered?

» Is transition support required for preparation for the world of work and independent living (as required in the IEP process starting at age 16)?

» Is individual or group counseling or psychotherapy required?

» Is parent education, consultation, or therapy indicated?

» What medical requirements does the child have?

» What are the implications of the report for IEP goals and objectives?

» What specific instructional strategies should be suggested for teachers? Instructional strategies should include specific interventions for treatment of autistic symptoms in the school as well as adaptive skills.

» What helpful resources are available for parents and teachers (webinars, DVDs, books, websites, courses)?

Features of HFASD Typically Addressed in an Intervention Plan

Common areas requiring intervention in HFASD are:
» social skills;
» executive functioning;
» language/communication skills;
» fine- and gross-motor skills;
» managing the sensory world;
» adaptive independence skills;
» coexisting psychiatric problems, especially ADHD, anxiety, and mood disorders;
» academic/work issues;
» behavioral problems; and
» medical issues, including pharmacological interventions.

General Principles of Effective Treatment Planning

Following a thorough assessment, a comprehensive treatment plan should involve a multidisciplinary team to provide interventions. These can be specific therapies or activities, medical consultations, or family supports. This involves active parent involvement and communication between all team members. When providers work with children with HFASD there are shared principles of treatment that should be kept in mind. These include:

» *An emphasis on generalization of skills between tasks, settings, different teachers, and the variety of treatment personnel.* If the treatment only helps a child when he or she is in the therapist's office and doesn't help in real-world settings like home and school, then it isn't much use.

» *Active involvement of the parent(s) in treatment.* This should involve parent education through web resources, DVDs, workshops, and guided therapeutic support, especially where behavior challenges are present. Parents should be clearly informed about what the specific goals of the treatment are and how they can reinforce and support the treatment at home. Parenting stress may require therapeutic support. Parents may require marital or family counseling.

» *Active communication between all team members including parents.*

» *The use of scientific, evidence-based practices.* Evidence based means that there is scientific evidence presented in peer-reviewed journals that the intervention actually improves functioning in some way.

» *The therapist focuses on building rapport with the child and family.* Parents need to feel comfortable with their therapist, and not just because the therapist was assigned to them by a hospital or insurance list or other impersonal means. Children, especially teenagers, need to experience comfort working with the therapist. It really helps if the child or teen client likes his or her therapist. It is, after all, the therapist's job to make the client feel that she can reveal her private self, goals, aspirations, and challenges.

» *A strengths-based model.* This means that the therapy explicitly builds on the interests and strengths of the child, and incorporates them into the therapeutic work.

» *Monitoring and addressing the child's stress in both home and school settings.* Identifying the child's stressful experiences is very important, because of the unusually strong reaction children with HFASD can display to unexpected frustration.

» *Monitoring and addressing the self-esteem of the child, which can be fragile.* This should be kept in mind instructionally and in counseling/therapy. Confidence and self-esteem should be goals for every child.

» *Modification of classic approaches to better fit HFASD.* We know that early intervention is very important. With very young children with intellectual and language challenges, Applied Behavior Analysis (ABA), or behavior modification, approaches are commonly employed and are effective. With brighter children and those with more language, ABA treatment systems may be less effective compared to those using the strengths in their cognitive and language skills (such as Cognitive Behavior Therapy or CBT), or ABA can be mixed with more cognitive/symbolic teaching styles. CBT uses more logical approaches to think through behavior choices.

» *Adaptive skills through the lifespan need to be addressed for independent living, world of work, adult socialization, and sexuality.* Adaptive skills are real-world, functional activities, like shopping and doing the laundry, that are valuable in everyday life.

» *Assigning roles and responsibilities in the multidisciplinary plan.* Everyone on a treatment team must have a responsibility and a job to do.

The Multidisciplinary Team

There is no one "magic bullet" treatment for HFASD. HFASDs are conditions that respond to multimodal treatment systems employing integrated treatments and multiple stakeholders in wraparound plans utilizing a variety of team members. In other words, effective treatment of HFASD usually requires a team of people with different specialties working together with the parents and the child. By "wraparound," we mean that most aspects of the child's life are addressed with a consistent focus on specific, targeted developmental or behavioral objectives. Although every person with HFASD does not require a wraparound intervention plan, multiple treatments often work in combination to make a difference. A multidisciplinary team is also interdisciplinary. It is not enough to collect a number of separate opinions by professionals representing different disciplines; team members also need to communicate with each other.

Case management is very important. Someone needs to be in charge of the communication. One-way communication between parent(s) and providers with little coordination of care often leads to confusion and inconsistency in treatment. Closely coordinated communication between all stakeholders, including teachers, medical doctors, therapists, and family, is especially important when working with children with HFASD, who require consistency across settings. Child rearing, especially for children with disabilities, does "take a village." Without coordinated efforts, telephone calls, e-mails, and texts are flying around between stakeholders with little shared information or sense of assigned responsibility. Too often, coordination of treatment for the child is completely shouldered by parents, who also act as case managers. In schools, hospitals, or other treatment settings, the planning should be coordinated by a case manager, and treatment shared by a number of specialists. In a best-case scenario, families work with team members who are communicating regularly and effectively with each other. This is sometimes challenging when treatment teams are compartmentalized as in some hospital or university settings.

The following team members from both school and private treatment settings frequently participate:

» parent(s);
» teacher(s): teachers and aids, especially special education teachers, should have competencies in the instruction of students with HFASDs;

» school administrator(s);
» counselor;
» psychologist;
» evaluating psychologist;
» treating therapist(s);
» behavior specialist;
» speech-language pathologist;
» occupational therapist;
» psychiatrist, physician, or nurse administering medication;
» physical therapist;
» assistive technology specialist; and
» the child (when appropriate).

The child participates in treatment planning. A coordinated plan works best when the child is able to comprehend it and take ownership to become his or her own advocate. This often includes understanding one's strengths and needs. Hospital or other clinical assessment feedback, planning meetings, treatment team meetings, school IEP teams, grade level teams, etc. should consider involving the child for at least part of all discussions regarding the child. Often, there are many treatment and educational goals. It is very helpful when the child can take ownership of a few pivotal goals, especially when these goals can be included in home-school contracts or other agreements where there are incentives for goal attainment by the child. Of course, there are parts of the meetings where the child should not be present, such as detailed disagreements about diagnostic classification, etc. In general, it is best for the child not to be present for disagreements or other potentially upsetting conversations. Also, explanations of the child's strengths and needs must be couched in language that is developmentally appropriate for the child to understand. Students are often coached on how to participate in such meetings and often do an exceptional job. The goal, again, is the child's ownership of his or her progress. Parents are often very proud to see their child participate in meetings cooperatively.

Family Support for Navigating Systems

The early identification of a child's problems, the search for competent evaluators, making appointments, setting up follow-up visits, looking for appropriate educational programs, and general planning can be overwhelming to any family. There can be a general sense of helplessness experienced by parents when there is no clear diagnosis and no clear path forward. Most parents are self-sufficient in making contacts and following appointments, but some families benefit from family or system navigators. "Family navigators" are people who have their own children with similar needs who help parents of children with challenges. "System navigators" are frequently paid professionals or paraprofessionals working within systems that support the family through the assessment and treatment process. Some of the better advocates are people who have developed thorough knowledge of their area of disability or that of the child and have come to terms with working effectively with systems. Sometimes parents of children with disabilities or persons with disabilities can be very politically effective in obtaining better services and opportunities for children with disabilities. Many of the advances in protections for children with disabilities have been spearheaded by family navigators.

Sometimes an educational advocate, usually paid by the parent, can facilitate a support program. An educational advocate can be very helpful when there is need to explore available school options, or if there appear to be barriers to implementing plans such as a 504 plan or IEP. Educational consultants can demystify the process for families, identify options that parents may not be aware of, and help tailor a program appropriately. Also, for parents participating in the IEP process, a large school team can feel intimidating. There are many laws, rules, and regulations for parents to understand. The process does not need to be adversarial with an advocate present in support of the parent, especially if the parent feels comfortable with each step of the process as the meeting progresses with details and options and opportunities for their child clearly explained.

General Principles of Therapeutic Treatment for ASD

Although parents can't be their child's therapist, it is good for them to know as principal caretakers in the child's development and, in some cases, participants in their child's healing, what treatment is all about. Children with HFASDs generally require a multiplicity of therapeutic providers over the course of their development, which typically includes speech/language therapy, behavioral therapy, occupational therapy, physical therapy, and psychotherapy. The following focuses on specific psychotherapeutic techniques that are effective with children with HFASD, which can apply across disciplines.

There is no one methodology, intervention, or treatment strategy that has been identified as effective and comprehensive leading to success for all children (Toth & King, 2008). Because of differences in each profile, treatment plans must be individually tailored. Psychotherapies, coaching, parent support, related services like speech and occupational therapies, and pharmacological interventions work together with school and community supports to ensure a safer, healthier, and better-adjusted child with HFASD.

The overall goal of therapeutic treatment is to help the child develop long-term independent living skills. In HFASD, this requires improvement in emotional self-knowledge and self-regulation. Introspection is often challenged in HFASD. Self-knowledge and judgment of others can be based on "black and white thinking." Children with HFASD, despite their seemingly higher intelligence or language, may have problems recognizing their own thoughts and feelings. This can interfere with the inward-looking approach required for talk, or "psychodynamic," therapy. The principles in Figures 1 and 2 are helpful in adjusting therapy to the needs of the child with HFASD.

Provide Concrete, Detail-Oriented Explanations

Because persons with HFASDs often learn from particular instances to general ideas (from an aggregate of trees to a whole forest) instead of globally, it is a task to help them see the "bigger picture" view of situations, rather than focusing on individual component details. When people with HFASDs "systemize," they may be collecting information in an orderly manner but not really integrating it. Problems with abstraction and inference must be recognized in therapy. It cannot be assumed that the child "gets" the gist or pivotal key idea. Parents and therapists can help the child form concepts by showing how separate examples of things are alike.

Effective Types of Psychotherapy for Children With HFASD

Cognitive Behavioral Therapy

Cognitive Behavioral Therapy (CBT) is a frequently employed form of treatment that involves strengthening verbal control over behavior through discussion of why specific behaviors are important and rehearsal of specific skills scripts that support those behaviors. CBT is often helpful to people with HFASD because it tends to be more concrete, explicit, and based on specific goals. It is also ideal for teaching strategies for becoming aware of and coping with unpleasant feelings, like anxiety and agitation. Because new skills are only effective if the child can exhibit them in real-world settings, and not just in the therapist's office, it is essential that families and school personnel be informed of the specific behaviors a child is trying to change and the strategies she is using. CBT is most effective for peo-

Toward an Effective Counseling/Therapy Approach to the Treatment Plan

- ❑ A coaching approach may be more effective than talk therapy for many issues and challenges.

- ❑ Both individual and group counseling should be part of any program as a best practice.

- ❑ Direct instruction and modeling of theory of mind should be employed.

- ❑ Video modeling can be employed.

- ❑ Other visual aids like comic strips can be used.

- ❑ Peer-mediated interventions may be effective.

- ❑ The "social autopsy" approach should be implemented (Baron-Cohen et al., 1999). This is a process wherein recent faux pas are analyzed so as not to be repeated.

- ❑ Target behaviors should be "field tested."

- ❑ Cognitive Behavior Therapy may be effective.

- ❑ Consultative parent counseling may be employed, and parents should be aware of specific goals of therapy and how to support them at home.

- ❑ Direct social skill instruction, practice, and review may be utilized in an individual and/or group setting.

- ❑ Psychopharmacology consultation(s) should be combined with psychotherapy.

FIGURE 1. A summary checklist of approaches.

A Checklist of Specific Goals and Targets of Counseling/ Therapy Self-Evaluation

❑ Self-esteem

❑ Self-advocacy

❑ Developing a vocabulary for emotional introspection through self-talk

❑ Dealing with anxiety, including self-calming

❑ Improving understanding of the thoughts and feelings of others and gaining insight into the impact of behaviors on others

❑ Planning, organizing time and materials (executive functions)

❑ Increased flexibility of thinking/decreasing rigidity

❑ Speaking effectively in real-world situations

❑ Reading body language

❑ Incorporating special interests appropriately

❑ Dealing with loud noises, sensory overload, and other environmental sensory challenges

❑ Dealing with insults or perceived insults, decreasing paranoia

❑ Dating and sexuality

❑ Nutrition

❑ Planning for leisure and quality of life

FIGURE 2. A checklist of goals of therapy.

ple with HFASD if specific modifications are made. CBT can be modified for persons with HFASD (Attwood, 2004; Lang, Regester, Lauderdale, Asbaugh, & Haring, 2010) in the following ways:

» Increase emphasis on coping strategies that do not require abstract language.
» Incorporate special interests into CBT therapy sessions.
» Use direct instruction of social skills. Don't expect child clients with ASDs to "deduce" patterns of behavior logically.
» Use systematic rewards (e.g., verbal approval, token systems) to increase the frequency of targeted behavior.

Many children with HFASD have mood disorders. Attwood (2004) has developed a modified CBT, called the Emotional Toolbox, to be used in reframing assumptions about life that lead to problems in mood and behavior.

Behavior Therapy

Children with HFASD can become disrupted when thwarted or surprised by overwhelming expectations or changes in routines, and some display challenging behaviors associated with coexisting conditions such as ADHD. They often also have high needs for control that are related to brain-based inflexibility and fear of being overwhelmed that parents and professionals may view as being oppositional.

At home and at school, there may be a need for behavior analysis and an intervention plan. Schools can request a Functional Behavior Analysis (FBA) of a child whether or not he has been recognized to have a disability. This is often carried out by a special education teacher or school psychologist using a school system form or checklist. Engineering control over behaviors is often challenging, requiring a professional. Certification programs and requirements have been established such as those for the Board Certified Behavior Analyst described in greater detail in Chapter 6. This can be a complex intervention, which involves identifying triggers and consequences for behavior.

Kasari and Lawton (2010) explored current trends in the behavioral intervention literature for children with an autism spectrum disorder during 2008 and 2009 and noted an increase in programs using parent training and community supports.

Pharmacological Intervention

When behaviors and coexisting conditions are continuing to interfere with education, despite the efforts of staff to provide adaptations, accommodations, and instruction designed to improve the situation, parents should be open to seeking out the advice of experts outside of the school building who may recommend other behavioral or medical interventions. Quite frequently a medical specialist should be part of the team. Currently, there are no medications that are approved for the treatment of the core symptoms of autism. However, the symptoms and coexisting conditions are treated, in some cases, with medication. At the time of this writing there are two medicines that are currently approved for the treatment of irritability in autism. They are Abilify and Risperidol. In addition, attention problems, impulsivity, anxiety, depression, and illogical thought patterns are all being addressed with medication with some measure of success in individual cases. Medications should be prescribed by someone specifically familiar with the HFASD population who is willing to monitor progress and make adjustments in kind, combinations, and amounts of medications. An expert in pediatric pharmacology should be able to explain side effects and benefits of medications, working in concert with other interventions.

Adaptive Training/Instruction

Self-care and other adaptive behaviors for independent living can be supported at home, special school programs, and in psychotherapy. Jed Baker (2001) suggested that, in choosing adaptive behavior targets of intervention, one should consider how functional the behavior is. Can the targeted adaptive behavior be applied in multiple environments? For example, for teens traveling alone without specific travel training, public transportation can be dangerous if the skills are not established. When training an independent skill, it is important to ask to what degree community inclusion results from acquiring this skill. In other words, what are the most important self-care and community skills that the child needs to acquire in order to be able to live independently, hold down a job, or go to college? It is also important to pick skills that have a degree of generalization between different settings.

Social Skills Training

Social skills groups have been shown to be effective with students with HFASD. They are not, however, a cure-all for every autistic symptom or coexisting condition. It is recommended that social skills groups include family and/or school personnel or provide feedback to them, as generalization from learning in a weekly group session to real-world skills is the consistent weakness of social skills groups.

Individual counseling can also be very effective in increasing a child's social skills. It may consist of direct instruction in rules and scripts for interfacing with daily situations. This approach has been referred to as "coaching." A social coach can also be very powerful in helping a child to decode social situations by concretely discussing what happened in a certain situation or in a movie and how the coach knew what people in the situation might have been thinking or feeling. Social skills should be taught directly, just like any other skill. The child should be urged to observe peers whose social skills he does or does not admire in order to learn how to act and interact in different situations. Encourage learning about social skills, for example, by reading books about how to make friends, how to initiate a date, how to behave in a job interview, or from watching appropriate movies, etc. Suggest opportunities to practice target skills in real-life settings.

Training in Self-Knowledge and Self-Advocacy Skills

Children with HFASD often need help learning to recognize their own feelings, needs, strengths, and weaknesses in order to be able to advocate effectively for themselves in a variety of environments. Self-advocacy also involves methods for dealing with teasing and bullying. Another purpose of self-reflection is learning to be accurate about how to interpret and react to actual problem solving in real-world situations.

In order to know one's self, one needs to know the language of emotions. This includes being able to use word labels for feelings. Many people with HFASD do not distinguish their feelings well and do not have these words. Feeling words may need to be taught directly. We have found that counseling groups have had some effect when a mental health professional and speech/language therapist work together in a group therapy setting, because social communication is a total package of skills involving both disciplines.

Training for Dating and Sexual Behavior

There are not many studies on the sexuality of persons with HFASD. Sexuality is an aspect of social behavior, which, of course, can be a significant challenge. It is very easy to get into a difficult situation or trouble, as there is often zero tolerance for sexually related social faux pas. To be effective, it is necessary to ensure that there is a good community support system in place to "run social interference" for the individual with HFASD. Persons with HFASD can get into difficult situations because of overly literal interpretation of language (e.g., "You can't get pregnant until you're married"). Terminology can involve more slang and subtleties of meaning. There are many changes in societal norms. Permitted physical touch changes as the child grows to adolescence and adulthood. There is a great need to improve Internet safety.

In a study by Stokes, Newton, and Kaur (2007), when compared to their peers, adolescents and adults with HFASD were likely to:

> » rely less on peers and friends for social and romantic learning;
> » engage in inappropriate courting behaviors;
> » focus their attention on celebrities, strangers, colleagues, or ex-partners; and
> » pursue their interest in a person for a longer time (i.e., engage in stalking).

In recent presentations, Peter Gerhardt (2012), who has studied this area extensively, suggested that persons with developmental disabilities are at greater risk to be victims of sexual abuse. He sees sex as an underresearched area of adaptive behavior. Gerhardt's research of the literature suggested that persons with disabilities have less information than others. He believes that human sexual education should be directly taught. For example, persons with HFASD can be subject to Internet fraud and are vulnerable to exploitation and entrapment.

There is a continuum of developmental readiness to learn sexual concepts, and families must be respected for their cultural standards of privacy and modesty. Masturbation may be the only realistic outlet for sexual release for some people with autism. Realistically speaking, these behaviors may need to be managed for the purposes of privacy, health, and safety.

Treating Other Psychological Problems in a Child With HFASD

Children with HFASD often have other psychological problems as well. Leyfer et al. (2006) published a study on rates of disorders in children with autism. To quote the authors,

Accurate, reliable diagnosis of psychiatric disorders in children with autism is of major importance. When problematic behaviors are recognized as manifestations of a psychiatric disorder, rather than just isolated behaviors, more specific treatment is possible. Diagnosis of a co-existing psychiatric disorder may qualify the treatment of a child with autism for coverage by medical insurance. From a public health perspective, rates of co-morbid psychiatric disorders in autism are an important consideration in planning for provision of services.

Leyfer et al. (2006) found that the most common lifetime diagnosis in their sample of people with autism was specific phobia (44% of the sample). The majority of children with autism had phobias of more than one object or situation. More than 10% of the children with autism had a phobia of loud noises, which is not common in typically developing children. The second most frequent disorder was Obsessive-Compulsive Disorder (OCD), diagnosed in 37% of the children with autism.

The third most common diagnosis was Attention Deficit/Hyperactivity Disorder (ADHD), found in 31% of the children with autism. The rate is increased to nearly 55% when children were included who had ADHD that was significantly impairing but fell just short of meeting full DSM criteria. Sixty-five percent of the children diagnosed with ADHD had the inattentive sub-type. In children without autism, the hyperactive type is most common.

Ten percent of the children with autism had at least one episode of major depression. When depression was significantly impairing, but fell short of meeting full DSM criteria, the rate of major depression increased to nearly 24%. Only a very, very small percentage (2% or less) had mood disorders or bipolar disorder, and none were diagnosed with schizophrenia. In addition, various types of anxiety are believed to be so common in autism that symptoms of anxiety disorders have been thought by some clinicians and investigators to be aspects of autism, rather than comorbid features.

Given the risk of coexisting conditions, there are many mental health risks facing adults with HFASD who have not received a formal diagnosis. It is understandable that if they are living without recognition and support for their disorder, then adults can experience anxiety, depression, isolation, and low self-esteem. Tantam (2000) described secondary reactions to the stress of coping with the disability socially, which included affective disorders, anxiety-related disorders, and conduct disorders. Marston and Clarke (1999) have addressed the problems of grief and bereavement experienced when a person with HFASD is faced with the loss of a loved one. Death is part of life, as is mourning. When individuals struggle with identifying and expressing emotions, the bereavement process can be difficult.

More recently, clinicians are gaining experience with adults. Some are finding that those who were seen as gentle, vulnerable, and subject to teasing and bullying as children have had psychiatric problems in adulthood. Some are finding increased paranoia with years of social rejection. Loneliness and extreme withdrawal place people at risk for isolated thinking, which means they are not "checking out" their interpretations of social events. This can result in distorted perception and thinking.

Wachtel and Shorter (2013), in response to the recent series of mass murders in Connecticut, Colorado, Norway, and elsewhere, described a pattern emerging characterized by young men, whose social isolation borders on autism, who have become prey to psychotic ideation, and who, under its influence, have committed violent crimes. They argued that in some of these tragic cases, two concomitant diagnoses might be at play, namely autism and psychosis. They note that autism itself is not an intrinsically violent disorder, and individuals with ASD are no more prone to violent behaviors than the general population. In their hypothesis, the additional presence of psychotic illness, however, may change the picture. They conclude that there may be a kind of one-two "vulnerability punch," giving individuals with HFASD a baseline higher risk of comorbid psychiatric illness. Recognizing the increased susceptibility of individuals with autism and other neurodevelopmental disabilities to concomitant psychotic illness increases the possibility that they can be correctly identified and treated, mitigating socially deleterious outcomes.

It is important to realize and remember that we are describing a very small number of people, some who have been neglected by society. In general, autism is not about violence as much as it is related statistically to problems of reciprocity and other core symptoms with coexisting attention, anxiety, and depression. The important point here is to support efforts toward early diagnosis, early intervention, support in schools and mental health systems, and community living for a positive quality of life for persons with HFASD.

It can be seen that persons with HFASD require highly specialized approaches to therapeutic treatment and professionals who are thoroughly familiar with this population. Plans need to be individualized for the unique needs of each individual to increase success not only in education, but also in quality of life in independent living and the world of work.

chapter 5

Best Practices in School

Shawn appears in his counselor's office during the second period of his first day in middle school. Overwhelmed with anxiety, he has wandered the school building, trying to find his classes. The noise of the hallways, with the hustle and bustle of movement between classes, has almost put him in a state of shock. It has been hard for him to formulate questions for other students or teachers to help him in finding his way. He feels completely overwhelmed by all of the new faces, transitions, and information. Trying to be strong, he holds back tears. He had already gotten upset as he left his first period class, where things had not gone well. Students had been called on to introduce themselves and tell about one area of interest. He didn't know why the teacher had insisted on cutting him off in the middle of his discussion of all of the Pokémon characters. Things had only gotten worse when all students were assigned to read a short passage and he was called on and asked to explain what the main character might have been thinking before the climax of the story. He had no clue how to answer the question. The loud sounds of the practice fire drill only contributed more to his upset, and finally, he was completely thrown off when he packed up his books to go at 8:45 a.m., the ending time for the class listed on his schedule, only to be told that this was an extended first period for the first day of school. By the time Shawn found the counselor's office, his only desire was to return to the safe, predictable environment of his elementary school.

Dealing with the typical school environment may prove to be very difficult for the child or young adult with HFASD. He may find school to be a place that does not seem to value or utilize his personal strengths and where he is asked to deal with tasks and an environment that directly impact his weaknesses or differences. Teachers may feel frustrated in trying to reach these students who are not able to perform when taught in the standard way, and these teachers may feel that they don't have the expertise to provide the range of strategies and interventions that these students may require.

The next three chapters will explore how the attributes of HFASD are likely to appear in the school environment. A philosophy that has been successful in working with bright students with learning difficulties, including students with HFASD, will be presented in this chapter. In Chapter 6, specific strategies that have proven to be successful in dealing with each of the major characteristics of HFASD in the classroom will be outlined. Tools that can be used by teachers, parents, and the students themselves to help overcome their weaknesses will be presented. The focus on school strategies will conclude in Chapter 7, with a look at the range of school options that might appropriately serve students with HFASD and a discussion of how parents can effectively access these services and programs.

As discussed in previous chapters, teachers and parents may be frustrated to see a child who seems very capable in terms of his or her knowledge of specific topics and may be an advanced reader and/or strong in areas of math, science, or history, but at the same time is unable to handle much of the higher level comprehension work of the classroom. The student may go on and on talking about his area of special interest, but be unable to write a coherent paragraph about the same topic. He may be a great source of information about a particular topic, but be intolerant of anyone, including the teacher, whom he feels knows less or is not completely accurate. He may know the daily schedule better than the teacher, but get thrown off by any changes and startled by any sudden or unusual sound or event. He may be extremely orderly with his possessions or collections, but very disorganized when it comes to his school tasks and turning in homework.

Of even greater concern may be the student's weaknesses in social interactions. This may be made more difficult by the individual's problems with understanding the subtleties of language and nonverbal communication, such as facial expressions or gestures. These difficulties with social interactions are especially evident within peer interactions, when the student overtly corrects teachers, and when he monopolizes the discussions. These social interactions may be a source of the anxiety, low self-esteem, and depression that are prevalent in children with HFASD.

The following is a summary of the issues that teachers and parents are likely to observe in the classroom in students with HFASD. We will explore each of these areas and offer strategies for helping students to deal with these problems in greater detail in Chapter 6. The issues, which we refer to as "The Big 10," include:

1. Problems with social interactions
2. Problems with flexibility, organization, attention, and other areas of executive functioning
3. Problems with ritualistic, repetitive, or rigid behavior
4. Need for predictability
5. Very focused areas of interest and expertise
6. Problems with sensory hypo- or hypersensitivity

7. Problems with language
8. Problems with abstract reasoning
9. Problems with motor issues including written production
10. Problems with anxiety, depression, and emotional regulation

Before entering into our discussion of the strategies that have proven successful with each of the problem areas, it's important to have an overview of the best practices for working with smart kids with learning difficulties, including students who have HFASD. Four areas of best practices for working with bright students with learning difficulties in the classroom have been identified (Weinfeld, Barnes-Robinson, Jeweler, & Roffman Shevitz, 2013). The four major areas of best practices are:

1. Instruction in the student's area of strength
2. Opportunities for the instruction of skills and strategies in areas affected by the student's challenges
3. An appropriately differentiated program including individualized instructional adaptations and accommodations systematically provided to students
4. Comprehensive case management to coordinate all aspects of the student's individual educational plan

Best Practice 1: Instruction in the Student's Area of Strength

It is clear that if students are to succeed in life they will do so by capitalizing on their strengths. Temple Grandin is one example of an individual with HFASD who has made use of her remarkable visual strengths to be a highly valued and productive member of society. For example, in *1001 Great Ideas for Teaching & Raising Children With Autism or Asperger's* (Notbohm & Zysk, 2010), Grandin described how her strength in drawing in elementary school "became the basis of my livestock facility design business" (p. xviii).

Schools must provide an opportunity for students to identify and build on their strengths, to learn how these strengths connect to careers, and to utilize their strengths to overcome their weaknesses. Adapting a lesson so that it capitalizes on the individual student's strengths allows all students to access the curriculum. Accommodating students by allowing them to utilize their strengths allows the students to circumvent their weaknesses. Teachers can use the student's interests to motivate them to learn things that are hard for them (e.g., let them work on written expression by writing about their special interest). When a student's strengths are recognized and utilized in the classroom, she sees that she is a respected and valued member of that classroom community.

Some of the strengths that students with HFASD typically display are a strong base of information, an ability to recall that information, a large vocabulary, reading decoding ability, a passion for learning, and a desire to share knowledge. As these strengths are developed, they can form the basis for a lifelong love of learning. When the student is assigned a specific role in a cooperative learning group that utilizes his strengths, he can demonstrate classroom success that builds true self-esteem and fosters social relationships. Unfortunately, the student may be overly focused on a narrow area of interest or interests. By allowing time for the student to learn about and share her knowledge about this area of interest, the teacher is again promoting self-esteem, showing the student that she belongs in the classroom, and gaining a valuable tool for managing the student's behavior. Over time, the teacher is also cultivating the opportunity for the student to expand and broaden her area of interest and to see how it may apply to a variety of new topics. The cultivation of the student's strength may also have a very profound effect on the student's future. As John Elder Robison (2008) described in

Look Me in the Eye: My Life With Asperger's, childhood passions can be the basis for future careers.

Best Practice 2: Opportunities for the Instruction of Skills and Strategies in Areas Affected by the Student's Challenges

Although we believe in placing an emphasis on strength-based instruction, teachers and other school staff must also provide instruction in the skills and strategies that are challenging to the student with HFASD. When the emphasis of the instruction is on the student's strengths, he will be much more willing to spend some time working on his areas of weakness. We owe it to the students in our classroom not to give up on developing all of their skills. For the student with HFASD, this means directly teaching him how to improve his social skills, as well as how to improve his ability to organize, attend to tasks, write effectively, comprehend advanced materials, entertain alternative points of view, and handle changes in his school environment. Teachers and related service providers will need to do a task analysis of any of the classroom demands that create difficulty for the students with HFASD and see where the student requires more instruction. It's important to note that it is not just the classroom teacher, but also a team of individuals, including the counselor, speech pathologist, occupational therapist, school psychologist, and special education teacher, who are responsible for this instruction of skills and strategies. In addition, school personnel should consider data from previous evaluations, conducted by experts within the school system or outside of it, to gain a full appreciation of those skills and abilities that are impaired and require direct instruction, as well as those that are areas of strength.

Best Practice 3: An Appropriately Differentiated Program, Including Individualized Instructional Adaptations and Accommodations Systematically Provided to Students

Although we have the responsibility to teach students how to improve in their areas of weakness, we must recognize that many of the weaknesses that we see in each of these students are directly impacted by the fact that they have HFASD. People can always be taught how to improve their areas of weakness, but it is likely that the core issues that are part of HFASD will remain as, at the least, relative weaknesses. Therefore, it is crucial that we provide the appropriate adaptations and accommodations that will allow these students to access the curriculum and utilize their strengths. Appropriately selected adaptations and accommodations make it possible for all students to function at their best and to not only have a level playing field, but to be provided an appropriate education and work toward realizing their potential. In choosing appropriate adaptations and accommodations, it is always crucial to remember that we are striving to move the student from dependence to independence over time. An accommodation such as having a student dictate her response to an adult may be very appropriate early in a student's educational career, but inappropriate when the same student has learned to utilize computer keyboards and organizational software. It is crucial that we measure the effectiveness of accommodations over time and either change or eliminate those that are not effective. Finally, it is crucial that all staff members who will work with the student understand the reason for the accommodation (Weinfeld et al., 2013). As students move from dependence to independence, they must be a part of this process, understanding their own unique strengths and weaknesses and learning to be self-advocates. Being a successful self-advocate means understanding one's own strengths and weaknesses, understanding what adaptations and accommodations are needed, and interacting with others to get what is needed in order to be successful.

Teachers who have learned about the principles of differentiation will be the most effective in working with this population of students (Tomlinson, 1999). These are the teachers who understand that within the same lesson, which contains the same goals for understanding, there are different ways for students to acquire the content. There are different learning activities that will engage different learners and different ways for students to demonstrate that they have learned the information. Teachers who understand this will provide the adaptations and accommodations students with HFASD need to be successful. The more that different ways to learn the information and different ways to demonstrate understanding are part of what happens for all students in the classroom, the less the student with HFASD will stand out as different. Universal Design for Learning (UDL) is a promising practice that can make learning accessible to most students without the need for too much individualized planning. The UDL educational framework relies on three principles to guide teachers as they use technology and other means to reach students with different learning styles, including (Rose & Gravel, 2010):

>> multiple, flexible methods of presentation that give students various ways to acquire information;
>> multiple, flexible methods of expression that offer students alternatives for demonstrating what they know; and
>> multiple, flexible options for engagement to help student get interested, be challenged, and stay motivated.

As described in the second edition of *Smart Kids With Learning Difficulties* (Weinfeld et al., 2013), UDL should be in place for all students, so no one is singled out or embarrassed about their differences. "It has been compared with making a building accessible to those with physical disabilities when it is built rather than trying to deal with an inaccessible building after the fact." (p. 120)

Best Practice 4: Comprehensive Case Management to Coordinate All Aspects of the Student's Individual Educational Plan

It is crucial that each student who has been identified as having HFASD has a case manager at school who is responsible for overseeing his or her program. Depending on the type of formal or informal plan that may be in place (see Chapter 7 for more information about types of plans), a special educator, the school counselor, or the classroom teacher may act as a case manager. The case manager is responsible for making sure that the student is both being challenged appropriately and receiving the appropriate supports that will allow him to access the curriculum and be successful in school, as well as monitoring whether or not the student is making progress toward achieving his goals. The case manager coordinates all of the school's resources and communicates with all school staff about the student's needs. It is crucial that he develops a partnership with the home so that there is two-way communication between the home, including parents and any involved community service providers, and the school staff.

This team approach will allow for all of those who are working with the student to work together in the best interest of the student. The case manager makes sure that the student is part of the plan, helping to educate the team about her unique strengths, challenges, and the accommodations that she needs in order to be successful. When it is time to modify or create a new plan, typically on a yearly basis, it is the case manager who takes the lead on coordinating this process. Whenever possible, as noted in Chapter 4, the student should be invited to be a full participant in the meeting. This may require coaching. When the goals or objectives are clear and simple and there is relative agreement among adults at the table, the student can benefit from being part of the process and taking ownership of his own progress. However, parents should know that having their child at the meeting is the parent's choice and there may be times that it is best for the child not to come into the meeting until the adults have had a chance to air any disagreements and come to a collaborative decision.

Students with HFASD, like other bright kids with learning difficulties, can be successful in school when these four best practices are applied to their school experience. Parents and teachers must work together to find ways to utilize and develop the students' strengths; to teach them how to improve in their areas of weakness; to provide them with appropriate adaptations and accommodations that will allow them access to challenging instruction, despite their weaknesses; and to provide case management that facilitates a strong team approach at school and a strong partnership between school and home. We will discuss specific strategies for utilizing these four best practices to remove the Big 10 obstacles to school success in the next chapter.

chapter 6

Strategies and Interventions That Work in the Classroom

In our observation at a public school program for students with HFASD, the day begins with circle time. The student repeats that, "it's important to use a lot of language," as he works on identifying the emotions in the picture of the face that the teacher is holding up. The teacher models excited emotions as she tells a personal story and each student attempts to emulate what she has demonstrated as they describe their own weekend experiences. The students work on keeping eye contact with each other as they take turns speaking. As the teacher refers to the visual schedule to preview the upcoming day, she prepares the students for the fact that today there will be an unscheduled surprise, and talks about how they will handle it. As she talks about the science lesson that will come up later in the day, she allows the students to talk briefly about their own independent exploration of their current topic of passion that they will have time to pursue as part of the day's lesson. It is clear that the students, despite their obvious difficulties with social communication, their difficulties with flexibility, and their own focused interests, are making great academic and social progress in this supportive environment.

In Chapter 5, we outlined the Big 10 areas that provide the greatest challenge for teachers and for the students themselves (see p. 83). In this chapter, we will discuss the accommodations that have proven effective in the classroom for each of these issues. These accommodations have been drawn from many sources (Alvord, Zucker, & Grados, 2011; Attwood, 1996; Cannon, Kenworthy, Alexander, & Anthony, 2011; Klin, Volkmar, & Sparrow, 2000; Magnusen & Attwood, 2005; Myles & Adreon, 2001; Notbohm & Zysk, 2010; Powers & Poland, 2003; Ralabate, 2006; Weinfeld et al., 2013), as well as from our experience gained in years of working with students in a variety of school environments.

Each section that follows also provides specific strategies to help students with HFASD overcome these issues.

Problems With Social Interactions

Social interactions provide a challenge for students with HFASD. There may be more than one process operating in social skills deficits. On one level, there is the ability to recognize emotions through reading faces, body posture, and voice inflection, and on another, the ability to make good cognitive judgments using the data obtained from this reading. Johnson (2004) suggests that social deficits may be due to a lack of integration among various perceptual and higher level abilities, as well as social memory or recall. Although students with HFASD sometimes relate well to adults, especially when they are allowed to focus on their area of interest or expertise, they tend to have greater difficulties in relating to their peers. Adults may be unaware that they are unconsciously assisting the student with HFASD by keeping the conversation flowing. Teachers may see the social skills difficulties when students with HFASD are assigned to work cooperatively on an academic project.

These social challenges may be more evident during unstructured times such as transition times between activities or at lunch, recess, or in the P.E. locker room. Even when the student's social problems primarily occur away from the classroom, they still may affect the student academically in that he may be preoccupied with the social interactions and may feel anger, frustration, anxiety, and/or sadness as a result of problems with these interactions. Teachers need to be aware that the student may be being attacked, humiliated, or taunted at times when the teacher cannot observe that behavior. Teachers also may see these students struggling with understanding the perspective, thoughts, and emotions of the characters in their assigned readings. Therefore, students with HFASD may struggle to answer comprehension questions related to their classroom reading selections.

In *Take Control of Asperger's Syndrome: The Official Strategy Guide for Teens* (Price & Fisher, 2010), socializing was one of the main challenges identified by students with Asperger's syndrome and Nonverbal Learning Disorder. For example, the authors quoted Sean, age 17, who described his feelings about socializing: "It causes anxiety when in situations I don't like. I have all or nothing thinking sometimes. I'm scared of social situations" (pp. 6–7).

The Medina City Schools (located in Ohio) program for students with AS will be highlighted in Chapter 10. They have had great success teaching a social skills program utilizing the Super Skills program developed by Judith Coucouvanis (2005) as a guide. Super Skills presents 30 lessons grouped under four types of social skills: fundamental skills, social initiation skills, getting along with others, and social response skills. In addition to highly structured, easy-to-follow lessons, the book offers a series of practical checklists and other instruments to provide a solid foundation for assessing students' social skills levels and doing subsequent planning. The following strategies and interventions will include many other recommended programs as well.

Strategies and Interventions That Work With Social Interactions

Protect students from bullying and teasing. All teachers and school administrators must create a safe environment for students with HFASD. Although bullying can take place at any school level, middle school tends to be the most problematic period. This is a time when all students are most concerned about fitting in and those who don't readily fit in are often targets. It is crucial that schools develop a policy with zero tolerance for bullying and teasing. Schools that have education programs that proactively educate all students about bullying and teasing have been the most effective in establishing a climate that is safe for all students (Suckling & Temple, 2001). A recent letter from the U.S. Department of Education (Musgrove, 2013) provided guidance to schools about bullying. This guidance about the bullying of special education students is extremely important for all advocates of students with special needs, especially their parents, to keep in mind.

The key paragraph of the letter talks about how bullying of a student can lead to the student "not receiving meaningful educational benefit" and calls on schools to meet to discuss the bullying and look at what other supports or changes to the environment should be in place for that student. Ms. Musgrove (2013), director of special education programs for the U.S. Department of Education, noted that even bullying that is less severe can undermine a student's ability to meet his or her full potential. The guidance goes on to say that, if a student with a disability is bullied, school officials should convene an IEP meeting to see if additional support or changes to the student's environment are necessary.

Anti-bullying programs, which are crucial for the well-being of all students in the school, increase in effectiveness when included in school policies that promote positive citizenship in general. There should be an established procedure for reporting and dealing with any incidents of bullying and teasing that do arise. It is imperative that the role of the "victim," a role in which students with HFASD often find themselves, is explored and that the victim is given help with strategies he can use to proactively avoid the bullying or teasing (Neu & Weinfeld, 2006). Teaching students who have HFASD specific strategies to utilize when they encounter bullies and having them role-play those situations can also be very effective. *The Resilience Builder Program for Children and Adolescents: Enhancing Social Competence and Self-Regulation* (Alvord et al., 2011) provides activities for helping students to deal with bullying.

Educate other students about HFASD and about the child's unique strengths and challenges. By educating classmates and schoolmates about the challenges of the individual child, a climate of understanding and support can be cultivated. The school counselor or psychologist may take the lead on this education and be able to present information in a way that is age appropriate. At older ages, the student with HFASD may self-advocate, as she helps educate her classmates about her own strengths, challenges, and needs. Temple Grandin, for example, recalled how important it was that her teachers educated her classmates about her strengths and challenges: "They not only explained the nature of my challenges, but they also taught my peers how to help me" (Notbohm & Zysk, 2010, p. xvii).

Some tips from neurotypical friends of students with HFASD to help other neurotypical kids know how to relate to students with HFASD are as follows (Notbohm & Zysk, 2010):

» Don't be afraid of them. Sometimes they act differently, but they're still kids like the rest of us.

» Ask them to do things with you or a group. They know a lot of things and are interesting.

» If it looks like they don't know how to do something, show them what to do rather than telling them.
» Make sure to get their attention when you want to tell them something.
» If you see them acting weird, remember they can't help it.
» They have trouble with all the social stuff, so give them hints or talk them through situations.
» If they're getting stressed out in a loud, noisy place, suggest that you both take a break for a few minutes and go someplace quieter. (pp. 296–297)

Utilize strengths and interests in cooperative learning. Teachers can help students to be successful in group learning situations by defining the student's role in the group so that she can utilize her strengths. When given a specific task, such as remembering facts for the group, students with HFASD can serve as valuable and positive members of a group learning activity. Similarly, their strong reliance on routine may help them to take on leadership roles in remembering the steps of the group task. Especially in the elementary grades, they may be the most skilled group members when it comes to reading aloud, math skills, knowledge of science and history facts, or demonstrating understanding of advanced vocabulary. Teachers also can set the stage for positive and valued contributions to the group, if there is a structured expectation for the student to share an area of personal interest or expertise that helps the group toward its common goal. Conversely, the teacher will need to structure the group setting so that the student with HFASD is not expected to socialize with others in a way beyond her current ability. Teachers can scaffold these social interactions by providing the student who has HFASD with some questions he should ask of the other students.

Rehearsal of group work time and utilization of social stories that help the student to learn about the expectations of the group work time are also valuable ways to prepare for this potentially difficult situation. The social stories method was first developed by Carol Gray in 1991 and periodically has been modified and updated since that time (Gray & White, 2002). Social stories present appropriate social behaviors in the form of a story in an effort to help students with HFASD learn how to deal with a variety of situations. The stories include descriptive sentences that describe what people do, perspective sentences that describe typical reactions to the situation, directive sentences that direct the person to the appropriate response, and control sentences that help the person with HFASD to remember to use what he or she has learned in the social story when the challenging situation arises. Gray and White (2002) emphasized that for every control or directive sentence, there should be two to five descriptive and prescriptive sentences. Students with HFASD need to be taught social skills such as reading social cues and using coping strategies in an emotionally safe environment (Marks et al., 1999). A commonly needed social story is what a person with HFASD should do if a peer says something that is incorrect or doesn't seem to them to be very smart.

Teach theory of mind (learning to understand the perspectives, feelings, and thoughts of others). Students with HFASD tend to have great difficulty taking on the perspective of another person. They need to be explicitly taught how neurotypical people think. This should be done in a way that communicates that there's not anything wrong with the way that the child with HFASD thinks. As Dr. Michael McManmon, the founder and executive director of the College Internship Program, says, "We teach our students that they are like Apple computers, when the rest of the world is PC" (M. McManmon, personal communication, December 2006). Dr. McManmon and his staff emphasize to their students that there's nothing wrong with Apple computers, but because most of the rest of the world has a different operating system, the Apple computers need to be able to communicate with the other operating system. (The College Internship Program is located in several cities across the United

States and provides comprehensive supports to students with HFASD, as well as other disabilities, so that they can be successful in taking part in the programs of the neighboring college campuses.)

Similarly, students with HFASD need to be encouraged to stop and think about how the neurotypical student will feel before they speak or act. Again, it may be the school psychologist, counselor, or speech pathologist who takes the lead in educating the student about theory of mind, but the classroom teacher certainly can support this effort by explicitly explaining his or her thinking and asking students to do the same. Students need instruction and practice in taking on the perspective of others and in empathizing with others (Alvord et. al., 2011).

Teach students how to read and react to nonverbal social cues. Students with HFASD need to be explicitly taught how to read nonverbal gestures and communication. They should be taught about appropriate personal space and about facial expressions and gestures that signal interest or lack of interest. They need to be able to link facial expressions with the variety of emotions that they represent. Students with HFASD can be taught to rate the emotional intensity that another person is showing or to remember a time that they felt the emotion that a facial expression or gesture illustrates. They can be taught to link the feelings represented nonverbally with movies, cartoons, or books that illustrate that emotion. When reading a book or watching a movie, teachers should discuss the character's feelings and tie it to the character's facial expression and other nonverbal communication. Similarly, students with HFASD can be taught to identify and label the purpose of the nonverbal gesture that is used by neurotypical peers to regulate social interaction. School staff can use photos or clippings from magazines to give students practice with facial expressions. Teachers and social skill coaches should also explicitly explain nonverbal cues that the student may have missed in real-world interactions (e.g., "Did you notice that she put her hand on her hip and started talking slowly? Those were signs that she was getting mad."). These types of lessons work, too: John Elder Robison, in a 2011 talk at Google Headquarters, spoke about how, by studying nonverbal expressions and their meaning, he is now able to be right 75%–80% of the time, when he used to "just guess" what people were expressing nonverbally.

One outstanding resource for work on reading nonverbal cues is a DVD called *Mind Reading*, developed in 2004 by Dr. Simon Baron-Cohen at Cambridge University, which uses video clips to teach students to identify emotions in others. Another great resource, particularly for younger kids, is Jed Baker's (2001) *The Social Skills Picture Book*.

Teach students how to participate in conversations. Students with HFASD do not only have difficulty reading non-verbal social clues—they also frequently have difficulties under-standing the rules of conversation. Again, they need explicit instruction to help them learn these rules. This is an area where the expertise of a speech and language pathologist is crucial. Specifically, these students need to be taught how to enter a con-versation, stop to listen to their conversational partner, shift top-ics, expand on a topic, and repair breakdowns in conversations by seeking clarification or assistance when confused. Teachers will need to provide some accommodations for students with HFASD in this area. Students may need a warning that they will be called on to discuss a specific topic in a few minutes. Teachers may need to use wait time more when calling on students, to give the student with HFASD a chance to formulate her answer. Students who ask the same questions repeatedly or who want to talk only about one topic may need to be given help in regulating these behaviors, such as a visual reminder about how many times they can ask a question and/or scheduled time to ask the ques-tion or talk about their area of passion. Students may also need help in ending arguments. Notbohm and Zysk (2010) provide a structured script for helping adults end arguments with students with HFASD:

Thank you for telling me how you feel.
I'm sorry you feel that way.
This discussion is over.
I'm changing the subject now. (p. 131)

When we talk about social skills instruction, it is important to break down social interactions into specific areas. The following are recommended conversational skill areas for instruction. Any and all of these could be included in the goals and objectives section of a child's IEP:
- » introductions,
- » greetings,
- » goodbyes,
- » eye contact,
- » turn-taking,
- » volume,
- » matching tone with the intent of the message,
- » giving compliments,
- » humor,
- » requesting,
- » protesting,
- » giving approval,
- » stating disapproval,
- » using slang in peer conversations,
- » explaining,
- » organization of social exchanges,
- » teamwork,
- » making supportive comments,
- » courtesy words, and
- » good sportsmanship.

Students with HFASD especially need help with how to participate in a conversation on a topic that interests another person, but that does not interest them. There are a variety of approaches to teach this skill. Students explicitly can be taught about the qualities of a "good friend." They also can be taught to observe other children to indicate what they should do. There are many different materials available for teaching social skills. A few social skills programs that have been observed to be particularly effective with students with HFASD are *Super Skills* by Judith Coucouvanis, *Building Social Relationships: A Systematic Approach to Teaching Social Interaction Skills to Children and Adolescents With Autism Spectrum Disorders and Other Social Difficulties* by Scott Bellini, and *Thinking of You Thinking of Me* by Michelle Garcia Winner.

In "The Social Communication Dance: The Four Steps of Communication," Winner (2013) outlined the four steps of communication that students with HFASD can and should learn. The four steps follow sequentially from (a) thinking about the person with whom you will communicate and everything that you know about his thoughts, and motivation; (b) establishing a physical presence with the other person that demonstrates, physically and nonverbally, the intent to communicate; (c) watching what the other person is looking at and his body language and facial expressions for clues that add meaning to what he is saying; and (d) using language to demonstrate interest in what he is saying by asking questions, making comments, and adjusting what we are saying based on how we think he will respond.

The Online Asperger's Syndrome Information and Support (OASIS) website (http://www.Asperger'syndrome.com) lists many valuable resources for the teaching of social skills, as well as for other issues related to HFASD. Students with HFASD can be taught social skills through dramatizing or role-playing a conversation, viewing or creating a comic strip conversation that provides a visual representation of the character's word and/ or thoughts, or listening to or writing a social story that features the appropriate interactions (Gray & White, 2002). Coaching is required to avoid social interaction problems and correct mistakes. Traditional talking psychotherapies alone will not be as effective as a very practical coaching approach. One social interaction behavioral learning strategy is SODA, which stands for Stop, Observe, Deliberate, and Act (Bock, 2001). Using the acronym SODA to help them remember the steps, students are taught to stop and analyze possible responses before reflexively responding in social situations.

Since the publication of our first edition, several social skills interventions have been identified as having verifiably positive effects on students with HFASD. The United States Department of Education's "What Works Clearinghouse" was developed as part of the guidance from IDEA 2004 that schools should seek to utilize research-based interventions. What Works Clearinghouse reviews methodology and reports on whether or not the methodology is effective, as measured by the Department of Education's rigorous standards. In February of 2013, What Works Clearinghouse issued a report on Early Childhood Social Skills Training. In this report (U.S. Department of Education, 2013), What Works Clearinghouse considered numerous studies and found two that supported the effects of social skills training on social-emotional development and behavior. The study by Guglielmo and Tryon (2001) and the study by Ferentino (1991) showed verifiable evidence-based positive outcomes when using "Taking Part: Introducing Social Skills to Children" and "My Friends and Me," respectively. Also meeting What Works Clearinghouse rigorous standards for having a positive effect on social skills for students of various ages were First Steps to Success, The Incredible Years, Early Risers, and Social Skills Training.

Another valuable resource for research-based interventions is the Association for Science in Autism Treatment. This website, http://www.asatonline.org/treatment, is especially valuable because it is frequently updated.

Teachers can provide opportunities to work on social skills in the classroom by incorporating opportunities into the classroom procedures. For example, students could be required to show completed work to the teacher, tell the teacher about what they had done, and then ask a peer to play, all before going out to recess.

Conversely, students with HFASD also need to be taught that, when they desire solitude, there is a way that they can have it without offending others. Again, teachers can support this learning by discussing and modeling appropriate behavior in the classroom. It may be the counselor, psychologist, or speech pathologist that takes the lead in teaching these skills, whether they are taught individually or in social skills groups. Social skills or friendship groups may be comprised solely of students who need these supports or may be a combination of students with HFASD and their neurotypical peers. These groups can provide an opportunity to role-play or rehearse social interactions. Do not underestimate the power of neurotypical peers to shape the social behaviors of students with HFASD. Interested peers, given guidance and support from an adult, may take on the task of helping the student learn more appropriate interactions (Kasari & Rotheram-Fuller, 2005). Peer-mediated interventions are not only cost effective, but they also place the social skills intervention directly into the relevant setting such as recess or lunch. This type of group has been described as a "circle of friends," and is described in more detail on the OASIS website. Students with HFASD can be taught to decrease their inappropriate statements to others by learning to whisper their thoughts or to "think it, don't say it." When things do go wrong, a social autopsy can be used to analyze the problem and try to come up with a general rule for future situations.

Teach students to identify, understand, and cope with emotions. Underlying the problems with social interaction for many students with HFASD is an impaired understanding of emotions. Students with HFASD can be taught to understand emotions by exploring one emotion at a time. Students can be taught to read and respond to the cues that indicate different levels of emotion and to use their visual skills to chart their own and others' emotions on a gauge (Bolick, 2001). Teachers can support this learning by using language arts lessons to explore how the character in the story, poem, or autobiography may be feeling and why. Students may also respond to journaling about their feelings if they are provided with leading or guiding questions. It can be helpful when parents provide school staff with information about activities the student has been involved with outside of school, so that the school staff can ask questions about the student's feelings while doing those activities. Students with HFASD can be taught to learn and apply feeling labels. Once the student learns to recognize when she is becoming upset, the next step is to learn specific coping strategies for feeling better. Calming strategies are discussed below.

Problems With Flexibility, Organization, Attention, and Other Areas of Executive Functioning

It is important for teachers to realize that although students with HFASD may be very focused and organized when it come to their areas of passion, they are likely to have problems with flexibility, organization, and attention that affect their work production in school. Students with HFASD have problems with all areas of executive functioning, but flexibility and organization are their biggest problems (Cannon et al., 2011; Hill, 2004). Dr. Martha Denckla (1994) identified the major areas of executive functioning as initiating, sustaining, inhibiting, and shifting. In simple terms, initiating means beginning a task, sustaining refers to staying on task and completion of tasks, inhibiting refers to blocking out other distracting thoughts or actions that are not directly related to the task, and shifting means moving from one part of the task to another or leaving one task entirely to move to another. The core issues of HFASD that we have described above, particularly the student's problems with social interactions and with very focused areas of interest and expertise, may impact all of these executive functioning areas. Problems with language, abstract reasoning, anxiety, and the need for predictability all impact executive functioning as well. All of the strategies that previously have been mentioned will have a positive impact on the student's focus and organization. There also are some interventions that are particularly targeted toward increasing executive functioning skills, helping students with HFASD be more attentive and productive in the classroom. Parents may also want to consult books that specifically address attention. *School Success for Kids With ADHD* (Silverman, Iseman, & Jeweler, 2009) and its companion book *101 School Success Tools for Students With ADHD* (Iseman, Silverman, & Jeweler, 2010) provide a menu of strategies that are effective in dealing with problems with attention.

Strategies or Interventions That Work to Deal With Flexibility, Organization, Attention, and Other Areas of Executive Functioning

Provide direct instruction in executive function skills. Just like they need explicit instruction in how to be socially appropriate, kids with HFASD also need direct instruction in executive function skills. Specifically, they need to learn what flexibility is and how it can be helpful to them, as well as to practice routines for being more flexible (Cannon et al., 2011; Kenworthy et al., 2014). It is also essential that these kids receive direct instruction in big picture thinking, goal setting, and planning, which are core executive function skills that enable a student to understand why it is important to be organized in the first place. Students with HFASD have brain-based problems seeing the big picture and integrating information (Kenworthy et al., 2005). They tend not to intuitively understand the value of goals and planning to achieve goals like neurotypical students do. Curricula like *Unstuck and On Target!* (Cannon et al., 2011; Kenworthy et al., 2014), which teach step-by-step routines and self-regulatory scripts for setting goals and making plans to achieve them, empower students with HFASD by improving their ability to follow classroom directions, stay on task, and complete independent work (Kenworthy et al., 2014). *Unstuck and On Target!* teaches the Goal-Plan-Do-Check routine, which is a universal script for completing any multiple step task.

As we strive to move students from dependence to independence, it is crucial that we provide them with tools that allow them to monitor their own level of attention, energy, and arousal. Many occupational therapists have expertise with programs like ALERT (Williams & Shellenberger, 1996), which aims to teach students to monitor "how their engine is running" and to self-regulate their "engine" by making appropriate adjustments.

Use visual schedules. As previously discussed, students with AS often will respond better to a visual schedule that provides for predictability, utilizes their strengths, and aids them in being more attentive and organized. The visual schedule may be displayed for the entire group, but also can be individualized for the student. It may be arranged vertically or horizontally and display activities by using words and/or graphics or icons in a variety of colors and font sizes. Velcro or laminated strips could allow the students to remove the item from the schedule when it is completed. Changes in the schedule for the day should be visually highlighted on the individual student's schedule. The student needs to know what will be different as well as what activity is not going to take place.

Use proximity to and prompting from the teacher. Many students with HFASD will work best if seated close to the teacher, so that they can be frequently cued, redirected, prompted, and rewarded for success. A signal from the teacher, whether it is a word or gesture, may help the student with HFASD focus. It is often helpful to combine verbal prompts with physical ones, in order to appeal to the student's visual strengths and minimize her problems with language. Because our goal is to gradually move the student from dependence to independence, we should always be looking at opportunities to fade prompts that are no longer needed. The distance from the child can gradually be increased and more obvious prompts can gradually be replaced by subtle signals or by general comments to the class that will also benefit the individual student with HFASD.

For students who need significant prompting, it is crucial for the teacher to first make sure he or she has engaged the student. It is only then that he or she can work on helping the student to understand the concept. Notbohm and Zysk (2010) offer the following strategies for getting the attention of some students with AS:

» Physically move to the student's level. Walk over to the child, sit, bend, or squat to get your face at the child's eye level.

» Establish attention. Get physically close, if tolerated. Put yourself in the child's line of vision, even if it means moving his or your seat. Watch for the student to orient to you—that doesn't necessarily mean he looks in your eyes. Be animated. Use visual props.

» Let the child know that what follows merits her attention. This could be a simple verbal or visual cue, a tap on her shoulder or arm, saying the child's name or saying a preparatory word or phrase, such as "listen," "watch," or "look at me."

» Use gestures and body language meaningfully. Avoid waving your hands around in the air while you talk; use gestures and body movement in a slow pronounced way so the child has time to make the association. (p. 62)

To ensure engagement, it is crucial that the student has completed his previous activity. For the student with HFASD, completing activities previously assigned may require waiting for a break, a completion of the old activity before the new one, or getting compliance to complete the activity by receiving a warning that time is almost up (Shapiro, 2006).

Structure work periods. Students with AS may benefit from having work periods broken down into smaller segments and having a clear definition of what they are expected to accomplish during that work period. A timer or stopwatch can bring even more definition to the time period. Being able to actually see the time that is left is helpful for many students with HFASD. Some tools for providing the student with HFASD support with time include an "hourglass," a kitchen timer, a stopwatch, a smartphone with a timer, or a wristwatch with an alarm. The website http://www.TimeTimer.com provides a variety of visual timers that allow students to see a red disc gradually diminishing as the time goes by. Some students with AS will need an adjusted workload for class or homework assignments. It is helpful for teachers to visually indicate where on the page the student is to stop, such as by drawing a line after the last problem or the last question the student is to complete.

Structure the environment. Students with HFASD may be able to focus better when their auditory and visual distractions are limited. Some students work best when provided with a study carrel or "office" in which to complete their work. They may need the boundaries of their personal space clearly defined, even to the extent of having colored tape on the floor to mark off the area. Other students with HFASD may respond to the use of an FM system that allows them to listen to the teacher over headphones as the teacher's voice is transmitted electronically via a microphone. The potential negative impact of both of these suggestions is that they may separate and make the student appear even more different than the other students in the classroom if he is the only student provided with this type of accommodation. However, for some students with HFASD, this difference would allow them to stand out less than their inattentive, nonproductive behavior may be already making them appear to others.

Utilize visual supports that aid with completion of assignments. Again, teachers should utilize the visual strengths of students with HFASD to support them in areas that may be weaker, such as organization. Teacher should post visual reminders of the organizational steps needed to complete a variety of assignments. Within an individual assignment, teachers can highlight directions and steps or mark beginnings and endings. Color-coding of directions can be an effective tool. Some students with HFASD will need reduced visual clutter on a page. Teachers may need to simplify the visual formatting of a handout or provide students with a way to mask all of the problems except the one that they are currently focusing upon. Teachers should visually model the steps that are needed for completion of the project or assignment, as well as provide a model of what the end product will look like.

Support organization with rubrics, study guides, and outlines. Students with HFASD and their parents and/or tutors, who are supporting them in completing their assignments at home, will benefit from receiving a clear rubric that tells what is expected in the assignment, when each part of the assignment should be completed, and what criteria will be used for evaluating the assignment. Students can then gain experience in monitoring their own progress on assignments and in evaluating how well they have met the expectations of the assignment. Outlines and study guides that specify what material is to be covered and where students can go to find additional information are very helpful to students as they attempt to learn course content. Providing written summaries of key concepts or a reminder of where to find those in the text may be crucial for students with HFASD who may have difficulty with conceptually organizing what they have been taught. Teachers can use the Bordering on Excellence Organization tool (see Figure 3) to analyze what organizational demands may be present in their planned lesson. They will make notes of the organizational obstacles in the middle of the frame and then quickly circle the interventions listed around the sides of the frame that can remove those obstacles and provide access to instruction for students with HFASD (Weinfeld et al., 2013).

Provide classroom structures that support organization of materials. Many students with HFASD will benefit from having clearly designated areas for materials within the classroom. This includes having clearly labeled areas in which to put their own materials, as well as places to put work that still needs to be completed and places to put finished assignments. A color-coded binder or pocket folder system can help a student to organize multiple subject areas or classes.

Utilize technology. Fortunately, there are increasingly technological solutions available to aid students with organization. Smartphones with organizers are commonplace in the adult world and can provide support to students with HFASD in organizing their tasks and commitments. Allowing students to take a picture of the assignment with their smartphone may be all they need to support their organization when they are at home. Laptop computers and even the less-expensive portable keyboards or tablets have organizational support capability. Software organizational programs, such as Inspiration, help students who are visual thinkers to web their ideas and turn them into an outline with the click of a keystroke. It is not uncommon now for schools to allow students to e-mail their assignments home and to e-mail finished assignments back to school. Students in our schools are becoming increasingly experienced and intuitive in the use of ever-expanding technology, and we can count on the fact that technology will continue to become more accessible, offer more options, and become easier to use. Parents should seek out educational professionals both in the school and in the community who have expertise in assistive technology and can help analyze students' strengths and needs and align them with specific technology tools.

Provide systematic supports for organizational help. Many schools routinely provide organizational support for all students. Providing a structured time and way for all students to record

Bordering on Excellence Frame—Organization

Adaptations/Accommodations

ORGANIZATION

Possible Stumbling Blocks

- following multistep directions
- planning the steps needed to complete a task

- organizing desk, locker, notebook, and other materials
- locating needed materials

- breaking long-range assignments into manageable steps
- prioritizing

Instructional Materials	NOTES:	Teaching/Assessment Methods
• visual models, storyboards, Venn diagrams, matrices, and flow charts • study guides that assist with locating information and answers • highlighters, index tabs, and colored stickers • assignment books and calendars for recording assignments • outlines, webs, diagrams, and other graphic organizers		• use short, simple directions • post class and homework assignments in the same area each day and assure that students record them and/or have a printed copy • verbally review class and homework assignments • work with students to establish specific due dates for short assignments and time frames for long-term assignments • break up tasks into workable and obtainable steps • provide checkpoints for long-term assignments and monitor progress frequently • provide homework hotline or structured homework assistance • provide a specific location for students to place completed work

Assistive Technology

- electronic organizers
- software organization programs
- audiotaping assignments

- e-mailing assignments from school to student's home account

FIGURE 3. Bordering on Excellence organization tool. From *Smart Kids With Learning Difficulties* (2nd ed., p. 153) by R. Weinfeld, L. Barnes-Robinson, S. Jeweler, and B. Roffman Shevitz, 2013, Waco, TX: Prufrock Press. Copyright 2013 by Prufrock Press. Reprinted with permission.

their assignments, including the use of an assignment book, can be extremely helpful for students with HFASD. Students with HFASD may need the added support of the teacher actually checking to see that they have recorded the assignment accurately. There also needs to be back-up systems in place, so that the parents of students with HFASD and the students themselves can clarify what their assignments are after they have left the classroom. Some excellent back-up systems include the use of technology—more and more teachers are now posting their assignments and grades online so students and their parents can access them at any time. This has huge benefits for supporting the organization of students with HFASD. E-mail also allows parents or students to quickly communicate with teachers to clarify assignments. Some schools even post assignments on a voicemail system, often called a homework hotline. Finally, students with HFASD can benefit from having the contact information for other students whom they can call on for clarification of assignments. Many students are already using instant messaging (IM), Facebook, and Twitter for this purpose.

Structure time during the school day for organization of assignments and materials. Students with HFASD will benefit from a daily time during the school day to learn organizational skills and have a chance to apply them to their current demands. This time may happen during the regular course of instruction or it may be a pull-out period or resource class where the student with HFASD meets with a special educator who helps him to review what needs to be done, how it will be done, and when it will be done. Students with HFASD need to be taught how to organize their time. Sometimes students may benefit from having an organizational coach at home who aids them and their parents in setting up a system for work completion. The diagram in Figure 4 illustrates one student's plan for homework (HW) completion for the week, along with other tasks on his calendar.

	Monday	Tuesday	Wednesday	Thursday	Friday
3:30 – 3:45	Break	Break	Math Tutor	Break	Clubs
3:45 – 4:30	HW	HW	Math Tutor	HW	HW
4:30 – 4:45	Break	Break	Break	Break	Break
4:45 – 5:30	Religious School	HW	HW	Finish HW	HW
5:30 – 6:30	Religious School	Free if finished with HW	15 minute break, then HW	15 minute break, then HW	Free if finished with HW
6:30 – 7:30	Dinner	Dinner	Dinner	Dinner	Dinner
7:30 -8:00	HW	Free if finished with HW	Free if finished with HW	Karate	Weekend!

FIGURE 4. Sample weekly calendar, showing times blocked off for homework. From *Take Control of Asperger's Syndrome* (p. 73) by J. Price and J. Engel Fisher, 2010, Waco, TX: Prufrock Press. Copyright 2010 by Prufrock Press. Reprinted with permission.

Problems With Ritualistic, Repetitive, or Rigid Behavior

Teachers may observe that some students with HFASD have routines or rituals that they do repetitively. Students who have behaviors of this type will, under the DSM-5, generally be diagnosed with ASD and not Social Communication Disorder (SCD). The ritualistic, repetitive, or rigid behavior may include hand or finger flapping or twisting, complex whole-body movements, or the persistent preoccupation with objects or parts of objects. Teachers will need to work with parents and other professionals to determine when and if to allow the behavior and how to minimize the impact of the behavior on social interactions and academic performance. It is important to realize that most of this behavior is not willful and should not be responded to as if the student was intentionally doing something bad or disobedient. Some of these behaviors may help the student to reduce his feelings of anxiety and agitation. It will be helpful to school staff to break the behavioral challenges into three categories: behaviors that are dangerous to the student or others; behaviors that are not physically dangerous but are socially inappropriate; and behaviors that are quirky or annoying but are not dangerous and not even socially inappropriate in all settings. There is no choice but to deal with the dangerous behaviors, but behaviors in the other two categories are more of a choice, and school staff will want to evaluate how much these behaviors are interfering with learning. At the Harbour Schools of Annapolis and Baltimore, whenever possible, students are taught to modify their ritualistic or repetitive movement into something that's less noticeable and fits in more with the neurotypical world.

Strategies and Interventions That Work to Deal With Ritualistic, Repetitive, or Rigid Behavior

Tackle rigid behavior by explicitly teaching flexibility. Repetitive behaviors are addressed in the sections below. Rigidity presents a somewhat different type of problem and is often expressed as difficulty handling unexpected events (e.g., a fire drill or substitute teacher), accepting the ideas of others, responding to constructive feedback, revising work, and handling frustration. Because they are biologically inflexible (Kenworthy et al., 2009), children with HFASD need direct instruction in how to become more flexible. The cognitive-behavioral program *Unstuck and On Target!* provides a curriculum for teaching children with HFASD what flexibility is, why it is useful to be flexible, and how to be flexible. It teaches specific self-regulatory scripts such as Plan A/Plan B and Big Deal/Little Deal, which teachers and students can use to help manage flexibility challenges. Preliminary evidence (Kenworthy et al., 2014) shows that explicitly teaching students with HFASD how to be flexible improves problem solving and classroom behavior and reduces rigidity in school and at home.

Conduct a Functional Behavioral Analysis (FBA) and develop a Behavior Intervention Plan (BIP). School personnel can conduct an FBA. Input from the parents is a critical component to any FBA. The FBA should accurately describe the behavior of concern, analyze the antecedents to that behavior, and describe the current consequences. FBAs should be conducted using direct observation, by school personnel, of the behavior of concern. In addition to the direct observation, school personnel may ask parents to complete rating scales or checklists to also help in the FBA. The purpose of an FBA is to inform a BIP. A BIP will help identify a common approach to changing the antecedents, to prevent the behavior from occurring, as well as changing the consequence of the behavior to decrease the likelihood that the behavior will happen again. Another critical aspect of a BIP is to identify a replacement behavior that serves the same function as the behavior of concern. It is very important to note that the results of an FBA may determine that the behavior does not interfere with learning, is not socially stigmatizing, and should not be a priority at this time. However, if a BIP is determined to be necessary, it is important to intervene consistently across people and settings. Additionally, it is important for parents to ask for data to be collected to help evaluate whether the BIP is working or not. It may be necessary to make minor (and sometimes major) adjustments to the BIP.

If possible, intervene before the behavior becomes established, distracting, or disruptive. Teachers may use a variety of strategies to proactively work on behavior. Counselors, psychologists, Board Certified Behavior Analysts, and special educators are all valuable resources for helping to work on behavior. Often times, ritualistic, repetitive, and rigid behaviors surface as a result of a stressful situation in the student's life. It is important to determine this quickly through an FBA so that the appropriate supports can be provided to the student before the behavior becomes established or is disruptive.

Students can be helped to rehearse appropriate behavior that serves the same function as the inappropriate behavior. For example, if the repetitive behavior occurred in order to get the teacher's attention for help on a difficult question, the student can be taught how to ask for help or how to ask for clarifying information. Social stories (Gray, 2000) dealing with examples of appropriate behavior can help students to prepare for positive behavior. Social stories use examples of appropriate behaviors by describing social cues, other people's perspectives, and a suggested appropriate response for the student. Using students' visual strengths by providing them with written directions and visual reminders of appropriate behaviors are also helpful strategies for students with HFASD.

Some students with HFASD may be taking medication for behaviors related to their diagnosis. It is important to note that some rigid and repetitive behaviors are side effects of these medications. Report these side effects to the prescribing doctor as soon as possible. If it is determined by the doctor, parents, and student with HFASD (as appropriate) that the positive effects of the medication outweigh the side effects of the repetitive behavior, behavior support strategies can still be put into place to help the student with HFASD.

Respond to behaviors in a way that will help minimize the impact of the behavior and/or extinguish it. Teachers who work with students with HFASD will need to develop a carefully thought-out plan that focuses on when to ignore the behavior, when to distract the student and try to introduce a new activity, when to reward the student for refraining from the behavior, and when to enforce consequences on the student for displaying the behavior. All of these aspects should be carefully defined in the BIP. Determining the best way to approach each aspect of the

BIP should be done in partnership with professionals who have expertise in ritualistic behaviors.

Need for Predictability

Teachers will see that any change in routine may be unsettling and upsetting to the student with HFASD. Students with HFASD need predictability and structure in their environment. Temple Grandin talks about the benefits of her "old fashioned 1950's classroom . . . where everybody worked quietly on the same thing at the same time," rather than "a noisy, chaotic classroom with thirty students, like too many modern classrooms" (Nothbohm & Zysk, 2010, p. xvi). Predictability applies to issues of time, rules and consequences, location, and who will be doing what. It is crucial that students with HFASD know what to expect and be given tools for handling any unforeseen, yet inevitable changes. It is not unusual for us to be observing a student with HFASD in a classroom and see that he is agitated and upset, seemingly for no reason. Then, we may notice that the class is doing some other activity, rather than the activity that had been scheduled for this time period. Often, this seemingly simple change is the root cause of the student's upset. Students with HFASD rely heavily on details or small aspects of situations in order to understand them and conversely often miss the big picture. A small change in a routine can be very upsetting because it throws the whole day or event into question.

Strategies and Interventions That
Work to Provide Predictability

Provide clear rules and consequences. An effective teacher of students with HFASD will strive to provide a predictable environment that includes clear rules and consequences. Visual reminders and reinforcement tend to be especially important to students with HFASD. In terms of the rules and consequences of the classroom, the student with HFASD needs to have a visual reminder available. It may be helpful to have picture symbols accompanying words. For some students, having their own behavioral checklist or visual system may be particularly effective. A visual warning system, such as green, yellow, and red lights, may be a particularly effective way of communicating to the student how his behavior is appearing to the teacher. As mentioned previously, the student may also keep his own chart that visually monitors or gauges his emotional state. Visual organizers work for both behavior and academic support because visual/spatial skills are often strong in students with HFASD. They also work because something that is visual is predictable. It remains consistent and constant and does not change until it is replaced with a different visual organizer (Myles & Southwick, 1999).

When the student sees more than one teacher during the day, it is crucial that she understands the different rules and expectations of each teacher and has an easy reference to this variety of rules. Having consistency among the rules of different teachers will be a significant help to the student with HFASD. Some students with HFASD will need to be in school settings where there is more than one adult in the classroom. In these cases, it is crucial that there is consistency between the adults and it may even be helpful to have only one of the adults give instructions for each individual task or project. It is also important to have the same rules and expectations at home as at school. Temple Grandin pointed to the "close collaboration between mother and my teachers" as one of the key factors that helped her the most (Notbohm & Zysk, 2010, p. xvii).

Provide clear physical structure in the classroom. Students with HFASD will respond best to a classroom that is clearly labeled with the locations of materials, the location of activities, and clearly posted information that includes schedules, rules, and directions. Having too much material on the walls that is not relevant to the student can be a source of overstimulation and confusion. It will be important for the teacher to keep a neat and orderly classroom that is easy to navigate and is predictable. The predictability that this structure will bring to the classroom provides students with HFASD the organizational supports they need and decreases their anxiety. As stated earlier, having things clearly labeled ensures that the student with HFASD can be sure that these structures will not change.

Provide a clear physical schedule in the classroom. Because students with HFASD depend on the consistency of routines, it is crucial that they know the schedule for the day. Teachers should provide a clear beginning and end time to each activity. Students with HFASD will respond best to a visual schedule. It is even better if the visual schedule is also provided for them individually. For example, the instructor may support the student's maintenance of a personal calendar. A personal calendar in the student's possession provides security as an organizational reference tool and as a ready reference source. This may be in electronic form as an organizer program on a computer, smartphone, or tablet. Also, the student may have attention problems that can result in copying errors when the schedule is found only on a board at the front of the room.

Prepare for changes and transitions. Teachers of students with HFASD will need to take care to prepare students for both routine and unscheduled transitions. Visually posted or individualized schedules should highlight the expected transitions between classes and during periods such as lunch and physical education. Teachers can help prepare students for transitions by giving a 5-minute warning of an upcoming transition. Transitions, when possible, should be kept to a minimum. Remember that for children with HFASD it may be extremely hard to stop working on something that they are in the middle of. Teachers can prepare students for unexpected transitions by providing them with a laminated schedule and making changes in water soluble markers. Alternatively, sticky notes with unexpected changes can be placed upon the schedule. Teachers should take care to explain to and prepare students for any changes by not only talking about them, but, if possible, visiting the scene of the change with the student in advance. Students may need to engage in calming activities or utilize rituals to help them deal with transitions. Students can gain skills in handling unexpected transitions by learning to deal with scheduled surprises. The teacher can write the surprise into the daily schedule so that students gain experience in dealing with the unexpected. Students can be taught to identify novel situations and to then resort to a rehearsed list of steps to be taken to deal with this novelty (Klin et al., 2000).

One of the most stressful changes for the student with HFASD may be the times a substitute teacher takes the place of the regular teacher. Having a substitute teacher requires proactive planning on the part of the regular teacher. For some students, having a substitute may necessitate having a plan in place for instruction to take place with another, more familiar staff member. For the times when there is no choice but to have a substitute teacher provide instruction to the student with HFASD, it will be crucial for the plans for the substitute teacher to include important information about the student with HFASD. This information should highlight the student's strengths and challenges, any individualized plans that are in place, and key contact information.

Provide structure for unstructured time. Unstructured times, such as the time before and after school, the time between classes, lunchtime, recess, using the restroom, waiting for the bus, and riding the bus, can be the most difficult parts of the day for students with HFASD. Teachers and other school staff must find ways to bring structure to these times. Students may need to practice the rules of these situations and have these rules available for their reference. They may need to practice appropriate behavior through the use of social stories or specific scripts for the different situations.

Students may be given alternatives such as leaving for the class change early or late, and eating lunch, participating in recess, or waiting for school to begin or be dismissed in a different location than their peers. Students may benefit from having an individual "peer buddy" or group of peers (circle of friends) to support them during these times, which also gives them the benefit of an opportunity to practice their social skills. Students who are having particular trouble at recess may be given an alternative place to go at that time, but then be introduced to recess, with supports, one day a week. Teachers can bring structure to unstructured times by assigning activities for the unstructured periods. The unstructured time may provide an excellent opportunity for students to work in their own area of interest. When this is not possible or practical, this could be a time that the student is earning future work time in her area of interest by demonstrating appropriate behavior.

Provide instruction about the hidden curriculum. Brenda Smith Myles and Diane Adreon (2001) discussed the importance of "the set of rules that everyone in the school knows, but that no one has been directly taught," or what they call the "hidden curriculum" (pp. 97–98). This hidden curriculum must be explicitly taught to the student with HFASD, particularly to the student who has to deal with multiple teachers. Students need to be taught the following:

>> How to tell when the teacher is happy with the student's performance.

>> What the teacher does to communicate that he or she is angry.

>> Which teachers the student can joke with and under what circumstances.

>> What tasks are most important to the teacher (such as tests versus assignments).

>> What upsets the teacher and what the teacher's pet peeves are.

>> What the rules are for talking in class.

>> How to ask questions during a lecture or lesson.

>> Who to see if they have a problem.

» How to request help in each class.
» When and how to turn in homework and class assignments.
» How flexible the teacher is regarding late assignments.
» If the teacher allows students to negotiate due dates.
» How assignments are to be completed.
» Where the assignments can be completed.
» Where to sit in the class so that there is easy access to the teacher.
» What to do in individual classes if he does not have the right supplies or has left his homework in his locker.
» What to be doing in each class when the bell rings.
» What the penalty is for turning in assignments late, being tardy, or missing supplies. (Myles & Adreon, 2001, pp. 97–98)

Very Focused Areas of Interest and Expertise

Students with HFASD have very focused areas of interest and expertise. Although these may change over time, at any given time these students tend to be fixated on one or two particular topics. They often develop tremendous knowledge and expertise regarding their topic of expertise. They have a strong desire to read, hear, or view additional information, as well as the information with which they are already familiar about the chosen topic. They also are anxious to tell others what they know about the topic. Teachers may see this focused interest as a distraction from the concepts that the teacher wants to present on any given day. Teachers also may see the student with HFASD as disruptive to others, as she insists on discussing her topic of choice. On the other hand, when the student with HFASD is engaged in studying her topic of choice, she is at her best as a focused, productive student. When she is discussing her topic of choice, she is engaged in talking to another person. It is also important for teachers to note that when the HFASD student is involved in reviewing or learning new information about her topic of choice, her classroom behavior may be at its best.

Strategies and Interventions That Work With Very Focused Areas of Interest and Expertise

Returning to our strength-based instruction model, presented in Chapter 5, it is crucial that classroom teachers recognize, respect, and value the student's area of interest and expertise. This area of focus can become a source of pride for the student, as he may, indeed, be the foremost expert on this area in his classroom. When the student can see that there is a respect and value for his area of interest, his overall motivation in the classroom may improve. Again, it is important to note that development of the student's passion for a particular topic and knowledge about that topic may eventually lead to that topic being a major in college and/or a source of employment (Grandin & Duffy, 2004).

Provide a specific time of the day for focus on the area of interest. Teachers can demonstrate their respect for and recognition of the student's special interest by providing a specific time of the day for the student to focus on this area. This scheduling not only provides recognition of the student's need to address his area of expertise, it can also help the student with HFASD to realize that other times of the day are not designated for that special interest. It is very important that students learn when to "turn off" their passion for their interest area. Teachers should communicate both the respect for the special interest area and clear expectations about the need to do work not related to the interest.

Help students develop their area of interest and relate it to future employment. Teachers can help a student to develop his passion by helping him explore the importance of his interest area, including the careers that are related to it. A guest speaker or a field trip to a related place of employment can have very special meaning for the individual student. Finding an adult mentor with a similar passion can also help the student see that her current interest can connect to a future career. John Elder Robison, in his 2011 talk at Google, spoke about his early mentors in his area of passion at an engineering company and how this laid the groundwork for his future career. Students may want to read about John's experiences, eloquently described in his books, *Look Me in the Eye: My Life With Asperger's* (2008) and *Be Different: My Adventures With Asperger's and My Advice for Fellow Aspergians, Misfits, Families and Teachers* (2012). On the other hand, for some students, their area of interest may be something that is not related to a career, but is a personal interest that is just for fun and may form the basis for a lifelong hobby.

Use the special area of interest as a bridge to other topics. Teachers can use the special area of interest as a bridge to other topics. A skillful teacher will find ways to relate other subject matter to the preferred topic. Similarly, teachers can gradually introduce related subtopics that expand the student's area of focus. Students with HFASD first may be asked to look at the differences and similarities in the related subtopic or subject of study. Teachers may also use the student's area of interest as the basis for learning good research practices and for practicing written expression skills.

Use the area of interest as a way to facilitate social interaction. Counselors and teachers also can use the focused area of interest as a bridge to help the student with HFASD connect with peers who may have similar interests. The special area of focus can become a way to facilitate conversation and relationships among these peers. It may also help the student to develop social interactions through the Internet as he joins an existing chat room or builds his own chat room or website devoted to his interest. Students with HFASD often make good tutors for younger students, if their areas of interest include academic subjects such as math or science.

Use the student's area of interest to help regulate behavior. Finally, school staff can use the student's interest area as a way to help him regulate his behavior. Regulated permission to read his book of interest, view his special video, or talk about his topic of passion will help the student with HFASD to relax and regain his composure during times when he may be feeling anxious, stressed, or depressed.

Problems With Sensory Hyper- and Hyposensitivity

Teachers will notice that students with HFASD may become irritable, anxious, and/or withdrawn, seemingly without reason. It will be important for the teacher and other support staff to explore the student's environment to see what may be causing discomfort for her and to consider what can be done to either remove the cause of the discomfort or minimize its effect. Problems in the student's environment may include sights, sounds, and smells, along with touch and taste issues. For example, Temple Grandin described how "the sound of the school bell hurt like a dentist drill hitting a nerve" (Notbohm & Zysk, 2010, p. xvii). She went on to discuss the "constant flicker of fluorescent lighting" as another major school irritant (Notbohm & Zysk, 2010, p. xvii). For other students, their hyposensitivity may be evident as their arousal level is continually low. We may see these students as lethargic, withdrawn, or unresponsive.

When dealing with hypo- and hypersensitivities, teachers will especially want to consider whether this is a time for accommodations or a time to help the student deal with the environment as it is. Providing accommodations may be necessary if the problem is severe or if the teacher does not have time to fully prepare the student for the environmental discomfort. On the other hand, as previously discussed, if we can give the student the tools to handle this hypersensitivity, we can help him to become more independent over time. Care should also be given to balance the student's real needs for accommodations with the fact that providing the accommodation may unintentionally serve to make the child stand out more from his peers.

Strategies or Interventions That Work to Deal With Sensory Hyper- and Hyposensitivity

Alter or change the environment to decrease factors to which the student may be hyper- or hyposensitive. The teacher, with the help of staff such as the occupational therapist, should analyze the environment to see what factors may be impacting the individual student with HFASD. When possible, the environment can be changed. For example, a student can be seated away from humming lights, fans, or bright sunlight. Fluorescent light may be able to be turned off and replaced, at least partially, with other lighting. A student may find less flickering from a laptop than from a desktop computer. Placing black poster board or construction paper on a child's desk, or choosing to use colored paper, may help reduce glare. For students who are sensitive to the glare of white paper, using off-white, gray, or pastel paper may help. A softer color than black ink or black type may help some students with sensitivities as well. An area with strong odor can be ventilated. In extreme cases, students with HFASD may wear gloves to avoid an unpleasant touch or work with a partner who will handle any difficult materials. For irritating sounds, the teacher may be able to minimize the noise. If not, the students could be provided with earplugs or allowed to listen to their own music to camouflage the noise. Some students may need a study carrel or more private area in which to work. Some of the students that we have worked with have had two desks in the classroom—one for whole-class instruction or group work and another, more removed from distractions, for independent work.

Lining up to move to a different area may be an especially difficult activity for elementary age students with HFASD. Because of the student's issues with space, it may be best to place the student in the front of the line, so that he can self-regulate the amount of space he needs. Alternatively, he might be lined up right after an adult or trusted peer who will help provide him with the needed space.

Work proactively to prepare the student to deal with his issues around hypo- and hypersensitivity. Teachers should preview with students situations such as fire drills or science experiments that they know will be coming up that may impact the student's hypo- or hypersensitivity. A social story is a good way to provide this preview. Teachers should look for behavioral indicators that the student may be beginning to experience sensitivities. Students with HFASD should be encouraged to report their own sensitivities or pain. Children with hypoactive senses may need stimulating warm-up activities before being ready to learn. Some examples include guiding students to put pressure on their own joints and muscles. Teachers should help students learn to advocate for and use their own accommodations to help with their sensitivities.

Employ strategies that serve to help the students to calm or alert themselves. School staff may see warning signs that the student with HFASD is on overload. These warning signs may included the child flushing, sweating profusely, or suddenly becoming pale; somatic complaints; repetition of some familiar nonrelevant phrase; or repetitive self-stimulatory movements (stimming) becoming more impulsive or oppositional. The school team will need to work with parents and therapists to understand the individual student's signs of overload. Many students benefit from an alternative place to go in the class to calm themselves. A beanbag or rocking chair may serve this purpose. Sensory input such as compression, massage, using headphones, heavy movement, movement breaks, rhythmic sustained movement (e.g., jumping on a trampoline, bouncing a ball, marching), chewing gum, or using a water bottle may provide a student with HFASD with the needed break or relief when he or she is experiencing sensory hypersensitivity. Although research on the effectiveness of these interventions is not yet available, many parents and teachers have seen the value of some of these interventions for specific students.

For helping the child who is hyposensitive to become more alert and energized, strategies include hand fidgets and squish balls, drinking cool water, chewing gum, pulling or kicking fitness bands, and movement breaks. Teaching children exercises or movement that they can do at their desk to deal with hypo- or hypersensitivity, while not distracting others, may also be very helpful.

Some of the things on these lists may be familiar and easily accessible to the classroom teacher, while others will certainly require consultation with an occupational therapist or expert in autism spectrum disorders. (See additional strategies in the next section on problems dealing with the regulation of anxiety, depression, and emotions.)

Problems With Language

Although the language deficits of students with ASD and SCD may be most related to social-emotional reciprocity and nonverbal communication, there may be many issues with the subtleties of language. It is important to also be aware that some of these students will have structural language issues, such as problems with articulation, phonology, grammar, syntax, and vocabulary. In terms of the subtleties of language, while a majority of fourth graders would understand the teacher's comment, "This assignment will be a piece of cake for you," the student with HFASD may be expecting dessert as a reward for the completion of the assignment. It is important that teachers be attuned to the ways that students with HFASD may misinterpret their comment or instructions (or the comments of other students). Some guiding thoughts about communicating with students with HFASD are to "speak plainly, speak in concrete terms, speak in complete thoughts, and speak in the positive" (Notbohm & Zysk, 2010, p. 84). For example, rather than saying, "Students who don't finish their writing assignment will not have reward time on the computer," a teacher might say, "After you finish your writing assignment, you will have your reward time," or, even better, "First you will finish your writing assignment, and then you will have your reward time." Speaking in terms of "first and then" appeals to the logical thinking patterns of students with HFASD. In addition, students with HFASD also have difficulty with internalization of language; even though they may know and understand the words of the teacher, they may have trouble remembering and using those words later when they are needed to guide their behavior (Wallace et al., 2009). For this reason, writing down instructions and expectations is important. Paper checklists, putting instructions on white boards, and posting behavior expectations are all key accommodations for the student with HFASD.

Strategies and Interventions That Work for Problems With Language

Avoid or carefully explain ambiguous language such as idioms, metaphors, phrasal verbs, and figures of speech. It is important to realize that language subtleties may be a weak area for a student who in many other ways is very capable. Teachers will need to take care to avoid and minimize the use of ambiguous language. It is also important that teachers help students with HFASD improve in this area by explicitly teaching the meaning of ambiguous language and preparing them to have greater capacity when such language is used. Students can actually gain understanding of double meanings as they work on understanding idioms.

Avoid or explain the use of sarcasm or jokes with double meanings. Although we recommend that teachers in the classroom not use sarcasm in general, it is especially important not to use such language around students with HFASD, as they likely will not understand the double meaning of the language. Similarly, they are likely to have difficulty with jokes that play on words, such as puns and double entendre. Because this type of humor may be commonplace with their peers, it is very important that students with HFASD be taught the multiple meanings of words.

Avoid or explain the use of nicknames. The use of nicknames may confuse the student with HFASD or it may appear to him that the person using the nickname is making fun of him by using a different name for him. He also may not understand that "Billy" refers to the same boy that he has previously known as "William." Again, he may need help in understanding that multiple names can be used respectfully for the same person.

Teach students how to find key words and concepts in directions and instructions. The student with HFASD may miss the subtleties of expression or emphasis that a teacher or other speaker may use to signal a key concept. It is very helpful for these students to have the visual reminder of a key concept written on the board or on or on chart paper. Teachers can also give students an auditory reminder to listen for certain key words. In terms of listening for key words that a teacher may use repeatedly when giving important instructions, students with HFASD can be taught how to do this through the use of a social story about the importance of trigger words. Students with HFASD can be taught how to use their own voices to emphasize certain words through the use of modified stress, rhythm, prosody, and pitch. A speech-language pathologist, as part of the multidisciplinary team involved in the student's education, may play an important role in teaching students with HFASD how to modify their own oral presentation, which in turn can serve to make them more aware of the oral presentations of others.

Problems With Abstract Reasoning

Teachers need to understand that students with HFASD may demonstrate strong skills, such as an ability to memorize, which may lead to advanced spelling, decoding, and reading vocabulary. This memorization also may aid students in having a strong base of factual knowledge. However, this recall of information should not mask the fact that these students may have difficulty with advanced comprehension. Teachers also may see that students with HFASD have problems quickly making generalizations. They need to be shown many specifics before building to a generalization. This difficulty with abstract reasoning may be particularly true if emotional nuances or multiple meanings are being considered.

Strategies or Interventions That Work
to Improve Abstract Reasoning

Break down the goal of the lesson into its component parts and provide supports. After completing a task analysis of the vocabulary, understandings, and skills needed for the goal of the lesson to be mastered, the instruction should be broken down into smaller units. New vocabulary must be explicitly taught. Skills that will be required to complete the lesson should be reviewed and/or taught, if they are new to the student. Finally, the key idea should be broken down into concepts that build on one another with the result of integrating the knowledge of the lessons.

Utilize "naturalistic" instruction. A May 2002 *TIME* Magazine article featured an extensive examination of issues related to autism. As the article reported in a review of the literature regarding education, although children with autism may respond to being taught basic knowledge through association and operant conditioning principles, students with HFASD need naturalistic or incidental instruction in order to establish generalizations and higher level comprehension (Nash, 2002).

Naturalistic instruction places an emphasis on accepting partial responses that are spontaneous, even if they are less complete; evaluating for understanding of key concepts, actions, and vocabulary; asking open-ended questions; and encouraging higher order thinking and applications of concepts, through questioning.

Provide appropriate accommodations throughout instruction. Teachers need to build into their lessons the types of supports students with HFASD need. These supports may include a repetition of the small units of instruction, all levels and types of prompts, preteaching of new concepts or vocabulary prior to group instruction, a reduced field of choice, tangible reinforcements, and peer and teacher modeling, as well as guided practice and reteaching. Accommodations should be individualized and gradually faded as the student demonstrates the ability to learn without them.

Provide adaptations to the way the lesson will be taught. In order to capitalize on a student's strengths and to minimize the impact of her weaknesses, teachers will want to adapt both the way the information is presented and the way that the student is asked to demonstrate her understanding. Because some students with HFASD have visual strengths, videos, plays, CD-ROMs, diagrams, and graphs all may serve as effective ways to present information. If there is a film version of the book the class is reading, seeing the movie first will allow the student with HFASD to better understand the book. Similarly, students may benefit from having visual organizers on which to record key points and make abstract connections. Hands-on learning will provide a greater likelihood that students will gain an understanding of the concept, as will the use of visual, spatial, or musical patterns that offer emphasis to the spoken or written word.

Provide explicit instruction to ensure understanding of the concept being taught. Teachers should not assume that students with HFASD understand the goal of the lesson. It is important that teachers explicitly state the concept that is being taught and the importance of each learning activity. Students with HFASD may miss the big picture in reading and concept comprehension. The following list of instructional strategies for enhancing practical comprehension can serve as a guide to teachers as they work with students with HFASD.

» Direct the student to the significant main ideas to be sought in reading passages by allowing him to take notes using highlighter markers or similar methods.

» Maintain a level of challenge consistent with the student's cognitive functioning level.

» Have the student practice listening for key facts and check frequently to assure that the student can repeat the main ideas once they have been identified in class discussion.

» Have the student practice inferential thinking incrementally, using one logical step at a time.

» Have the student practice judging the relevancy of information through the use of embedded distracters.

» Ask the student to predict what may happen next in a story sequence.

» Ask the student to recall sequences of detail in a story or visual presentation.

» Ask the student to identify self-contradictions in material.

» Help the student to find similarities through classification of items.

» Have the student practice practical judgment for decision making in real-life situations (i.e., "What would you do if _____ happened?").

» Ask the student to identify the supporting details in an identified key concept.

» Ask the student to arrange or rearrange events from a story in sequential order.

» Ask the student to differentiate fact from opinion.

» Teach the student to locate information using a table, index, dictionary, or online search.

Move from specifics to generalizations. Students with HFASD may do best with inductive reasoning, moving from the parts of a concept to the whole. Teachers should begin with specifics and gradually move to generalizations. A unifying theme will help the student to find the commonality in the pieces of information they are learning. Teachers cannot assume that students with HFASD will make this intellectual leap without explicitly discussing connections between the pieces and the whole puzzle.

Provide alternative ways for students to demonstrate understanding that allow them to utilize their strengths. Teachers will have the most success with students with a variety of learning challenges, including HFASD, when they realize that there are different, yet equally acceptable ways for students to demonstrate understanding. Students with visual strengths may do best to demonstrate their understanding with a visual modality such as a project, diagram, or slideshow presentation. Students with auditory strengths may do best to present the information orally. When testing students with HFASD's acquisition of new knowledge, it may be helpful to have them do brief oral or written summaries of what they have learned after an activity is completed. It may be best to break down test questions so that they elicit one piece of specific information. Finally, it is important to be open to alternative strategies that the individual student may develop. Teachers should examine whether the student is using an alternative strategy and aid her in developing that strategy.

Problems With Motor Issues, Including Written Production

Teachers will notice that many students with HFASD have either fine and/or gross motor issues. These issues may interfere with a variety of physical requirements of the school day including physical education and recess, other activities that involve movement, and self-care. In terms of the academic expectations of the classroom, motor issues may especially impact students when they are required to perform written tasks, whether those are the writing of words or numbers. Teachers may want to seek out the expertise of related service providers, such as physical therapists or occupational therapists, who can provide specific instruction to the student and strategies that the teachers may employ to improve the student's ability to access typical learning activities throughout the school day. It is important to keep in mind that we are preparing students for a world that relies more and more upon the use of technology. Although we offer some solutions for helping students with their handwriting below, we believe that emphasis should be placed on having students with handwriting problems gain expertise with the technology that will allow them to communicate their ideas without being held back by their motor issues.

Strategies and Interventions That Work to Deal With Motor Issues Including Written Production

Provide support with and alternatives to physical education and recess. Physical education and recess may be challenging times for students with HFASD, both because of their problems with fine and gross motor skills and because of other issues, especially their social issues. Competitive sports may be particularly difficult for students with HFASD. Students with HFASD may need these periods of the day adapted in ways that ensure they are being asked to do activities in which they can be successful. Some students with HFASD may need a separate period of adaptive physical education instruction that focuses on developing the skills that they are lacking.

Although schools don't typically think of providing support with recess, without any support this may be the worst time of the day for a student with HFASD, who may need an adult to help structure activities and make sure the level of physical demand is appropriate. If this support is not possible, it may be necessary to provide an alternative, safe place for the student with HFASD to go during recess.

Support in acquiring written language skills. Students with HFASD may need very targeted and specific instruction in order to improve their handwriting ability. This instruction may include specific directions about how to hold writing implements and the paper, as well as instruction in the formation of the letters. A structured, supportive handwriting approach, such as Handwriting Without Tears, created by Jan Olsen, can help provide this instruction. Handwriting Without Tears is a developmental program that offers basic exercises in figure-ground discrimination and top-to-bottom and left-to-right sequencing.

Provide tools that allow for improvement of handwriting. Students may benefit from a variety of tools that ease problems related to handwriting. Some helpful tools include special paper with raised or clearly marked lines, edges of the paper that are clearly marked, pencil grips, mechanical pencils for students who press too hard, markers that require minimal pressure for students who press too lightly, and the use of graph paper or vertically lined paper to help with written organization in math. An occupational therapist can help with access to these materials, as well as offer additional suggestions.

Provide alternatives that allow students to write more easily or circumvent writing. First and foremost, teachers need to analyze whether or not writing is really the goal of the lesson. There will be times when a written activity is the actual goal, but in many other cases, writing is only one of many ways to learn and demonstrate understanding. When writing is not the goal of the lesson, students with HFASD should be allowed and encouraged to demonstrate understanding in alternative ways, such as creating a diagram, graph, or model, or drawing scenes (storyboarding). When note taking is required, students may be provided with a set of the teacher's notes or another student may be asked to use NCR (no carbon required) paper, which automatically produces a second set of notes that can be given to the student with HFASD. Teachers may find the Bordering on Excellence Writing tool (see Figure 5) an effective way to analyze their lessons and see what obstacles involving written language may be inherent in their planned instruction. After analyzing the lesson and making notes of the obstacles in the middle of the "border," teachers can then quickly circle the interventions that will remove the obstacles and allow the student with HFASD access to the instruction.

Allow and encourage students to use technology as an alternative to handwriting. Ever-improving assistive technology programs in schools provide students with many alternatives for expressing their ideas and demonstrating their understanding. Students with HFASD can work on a word processor or portable keyboard, many of which have built-in programs for checking spelling and grammar. Software programs, such as Co-Writer and Word Q, allow a student to type the first letters of a word and then see choices of the word she may be trying to write. Read aloud tools, such as Cowriter, WordQ, or the free Natural Reader can be paired with word processing programs, allowing the student's writing to be read to her so she can see if, in fact, she has written what she intended. Inspiration allows students to move from ideas presented visually to written compositions. PowerPoint and Prezi allow students to create a presentation of their ideas, focusing on their visual skills. A Live Scribe pen allows students to make a notation or even a symbol on special paper and later when the student places the pen on that notation, he is able to hear the lecture or class discussion that corresponds to his note. It is very important to provide adequate time for students to practice their keyboarding skills and to practice using the software programs before making a conclusion about whether or not the technology provides effective alternatives for text production. Sometimes adults can wrongly conclude that a program is not effective without giving students the instruction and practice time they need in order to be comfortable with the technology.

Bordering on Excellence Frame—Writing

Adaptations/Accommodations

WRITING

Possible Stumbling Blocks

- the physical act of putting words on paper
- handwriting
- generating topics
- formulating topic sentences

- combining words into meaningful sentences
- using language mechanics effectively (e.g., grammar, punctuation, spelling)

- organizing sentences and incorporating adequate details and support statements into organized paragraphs
- revising and editing

Instructional Materials	NOTES:	Teaching/Assessment Methods
• step-by-step written directions • a proofreading checklist • scoring rubrics, models, and anchor papers for students to evaluate their own work • graphic organizers • guides such as story starters, webs, story charts, outlines • dictionaries, word banks, and thesauri • personal dictionaries of misused and misspelled words • highlighter to indicate errors/corrections • copy of teacher notes or of another student's notes (NCR paper) • pencil grips • paper with raised lines • mechanical pencils • slant board		• focus on content rather than mechanics • focus on quality rather than quantity • begin with storyboards, guided imagery, dramatization, or projects before the writing process • set important purposes for writing, such as writing for publication, writing to an expert, or writing to a famous person • allow students to write in area of interest or expertise • allow students to demonstrate understanding through alternative methods/products • reduce or alter written requirements • break down assignments into smaller, manageable parts • additional time • work with partners or small groups to confer for revising, editing, and proofreading

Assistive Technology

- voice recognition software
- organizational software
- electronic spellers and dictionaries
- tape recorder for student dictation and then transcription

- computer word processor with spelling and grammar checker or talking word processor
- portable keyboards
- word prediction software

- programs that allow writing to be read aloud
- programs that provide for audio spell checker, word prediction, and homophone distinction

FIGURE 5. Bordering on Excellence writing tool. From *Smart Kids With Learning Difficulties* (2nd ed., p. 151) by R. Weinfeld, L. Barnes-Robinson, S. Jeweler, and B. Roffman Shevitz, 2013, Waco, TX: Prufrock Press. Copyright 2013 by Prufrock Press. Reprinted with permission.

Problems With Anxiety, Depression, and Emotional Regulation

It is not hard to imagine that students who are bright and who are able to see that they are having trouble with both the academic and social demands of the school environment would experience difficulties with their emotional regulation. Teachers may notice signs of anxiety and depression as students antici-pate, attempt to cope with, and then react to, their problems in the classroom and school. Although the DSM-5 does not spe-cifically list emotional issues as an indicator of ASD, these issues have been discussed in previous chapters and are often present in students with HFASD. Ideally, staff will incorporate other strat-egies that we have previously mentioned in a proactive way, so that students do not become emotionally upset. But, despite the best efforts of parents and teachers, students will become anxious or depressed at times. It is then crucial that parents and teachers observe and identify the signs of distress early and intervene.

Strategies or Interventions That Work With
Anxiety, Depression, and Emotional Regulation

Work to proactively minimize situations that will cause emotional problems. School staff should work together with parents to identify triggers for behavioral problems. An informal or formal Functional Behavioral Analysis (FBA) can be designed to take a systematic look at the antecedents of the behavior, the behavior itself, and the consequences that typically follow. After a detailed analysis of the current behavior, a Behavior Intervention Plan (BIP) can be devised to help to structure the environment in a way that promotes individual student success, while pro-viding a systematic response to the behavior and an opportu-nity to learn new prosocial behaviors. For individual students, their day may need to be structured so that they avoid crowded or noisy places. Alternatively, some students may need to leave crowded or noisy places early before they become overly anxious.

Students can be given permission to move through halls early or late if these situations produce anxiety. Some students will also need help to become progressively "desensitized" to the offending noise, sight, or odor.

Although behavior problems are not unusual at home and at school, they are not always a major presenting problem in HFASD. Negative behavioral outbursts are most frequently related to frustration, being thwarted, or difficulties in compliance when a particularly rigid response pattern has been challenged or interrupted. What seems like disobedience may often be sensory sensitivities, problems with social thinking, or other challenges related to the child's disability. It's important for the teacher to analyze the environment. Have we forgotten to offer a needed accommodation? Has the schedule changed without the student receiving warning? It's also important for teachers to ask themselves whether or not the child understands the rules and can remember those rules at this time. Temple Grandin talked about the importance of seeing the difference between a voluntary tantrum and an involuntary meltdown (Notbohm & Zysk, 2010). Your response to an involuntary meltdown should focus more on the support that the child needs and what you can do proactively next time to help prevent this situation, rather than on any consequences. Kenworthy et al. (2014) gave specific ideas for detecting and avoiding overload/meltdowns in students with HFASD, such as limiting exposure to large chaotic settings and becoming aware of the specific signs the child gives when she is becoming overloaded.

When thinking about consequences, we suggest that you think about allowing the child to experience the natural consequence when possible. When natural consequences aren't present, you may want to think about creating logical consequences that are closely tied to the behavioral infraction. When consequences are given, they should be given consistently by all adults who work with the child. Again, when giving consequences, you need to first always look at what caused the problem and whether you, as the adult, need to change something in the environment. Second, you need to analyze whether there are skills that the student needs to be taught or retaught that would allow him to better comply with the expectations of the classroom.

Cannon et al. (2011) have developed a very powerful tool for thinking about the behaviors of students with HFASD. Teachers and parents are encouraged to think about if the behavior is a "won't" or a "can't":

>> Is it oppositional, stubborn OR difficulty with flexibility?
>> Is it lazy OR difficulty initiating and shifting?
>> Is it self-centered OR poor social interactions?
>> Is it incontrollable outbursts OR overload?
>> Is it work refusal OR motor and organization problems?
>> Is it insensitivity OR difficulty reading social cues?

Identify signs of stress and/or overstimulation early and intervene before the problem becomes overwhelming. School staff should be aware of particular signs that show that an individual student is becoming anxious or depressed. These signs may include behaviors such as covering or plugging ears, squeezing body parts, or an increase in repetitive behaviors such as rocking or picking at one's skin, but they can be different for every student with HFASD. When staff sees these signs, they should intervene and provide an alternative and/or calming activity. Remember that interventions that are used for calming should be practiced when the student is not feeling anxious, so that the student can become familiar and comfortable with the intervention. School staff should be aware that the student may be overloaded after having to deal with the demands of the classroom, especially when there are many demands for social interaction without any relief.

Allow and encourage students to employ techniques that will allow for self-calming and regaining emotional control. Some typical strategies that can be put into place include providing periodic breaks; providing students with a checklist of steps for self-calming; providing a visual signal to students to be aware of their behavior and to use their calming techniques; teaching students how to ask for help, sometimes using an agreed-upon signal; using sensory techniques such as those discussed in the section on dealing with hypo- or hypersensitivity; allowing the student to listen to calming music; allowing students to refer to words that help them to calm down; and allowing students do a favorite activity. Other calming techniques the student can employ on his own include relaxation, deep breathing, guided visualization, or meditation. Students may even have access to their own sensory kit for calming that includes things like, "a small soft pillow, an iPod, several beanbags, a stress ball, chewing gum or chew necklace or bracelet . . . a handkerchief and favorite aromatherapy oil" (Notbohm & Zysk, 2010, p. 34).

Allow students to move to a special area in the classroom or building. Students may also need to move to a special area in the room or building, for a quiet time away from noises, lights, and people. In this special area, they may utilize sensory integration equipment and/or interact with specially trained staff. Depending on the program, this area may be within the classroom or in another part of the school building. If the student is moving to another part of the school building, it is crucial that there be a special educator, counselor, or psychologist there to help the student work through his issues. Students will need to learn what they need to say or do in order to access a break or a move to a special area. Many students with HFASD carry a flash pass that they can show to the teacher as they move to their special area. School staff and parents should remember that this type of "time away" from instruction is not the same type of "timeout" that we might use for a student who has been "misbehaving." This "time away" is not punitive in any way. Instead it is a strategy for helping the student to regain her composure and be able to return to instruction.

Help students to gain skills in monitoring and responding to their own behavior. Students may use a visual system such as a behavioral chart or "stress thermometer" to monitor where they are in terms of their own level of stress or discomfort. Students can also give themselves scores on a behavioral contract and earn extra points when their scores match up with the staff member's view of how they are doing. Students will also benefit from being taught how to handle conflicts and feelings of anger, frustration, or anxiety. Kelso's Choice provides nine alternative ways for students to deal with any conflict (http://kelsoschoice.com). Students with HFASD may need to be taught ways to communicate their feelings about times when they feel treated unfairly.

Due to their black and white thinking, students with HFASD may overly focus on what they can't do. School staff can encourage positive thinking by having the student keep a journal about "one good thing that happened today." Teachers and parents can also share the student's success by writing about at least one good thing that happened each day in her school to home and home to school communication notebook. It is also important to model and communicate the fact that everyone makes mistakes and that everyone needs help.

Teach students to prepare for stressful, overstimulating, and uncomfortable situations. Students can preview difficult situations by using social stories (Gray & White, 2002). A social skills lesson can also preview difficult situations and provide students an opportunity to discuss and role-play how they will handle it. For example, a community outing, such as a field trip, can be rehearsed ahead of time. The mode of transportation and route can be researched before the trip. Anticipated interactions can be scripted and practiced. The components of potentially stressful situations can be generalized into rules that can be practiced and learned.

Consider medication with a psychiatrist or pediatrician. When behaviors are continuing to interfere with education, despite the efforts of staff to provide adaptations, accommodations, and instruction designed to improve the situation, parents should be open to seeking out the advice of experts outside of the school building who may recommend other behavioral or medical interventions. Medications are discussed in Chapter 4.

Consider behavioral consultation with a behavior intervention specialist. Parents may want to involve a behavior intervention specialist, particularly a Board Certified Behavior Analyst (BCBA). A BCBA can conduct assessments and provide applied behavior analytic interventions that are based on published research for both the home and school. These plans typically focus on the acquisition of skills, such as social skills or coping skills, as well as specific ways to reduce challenging behaviors. Additionally, BCBAs can assess whether a challenging behavior is occurring due to the lack of generalization or skill transfer from one situation to another. For example, often times, students with HFASD will be able to complete an assignment in one classroom but not in another. BCBAs can also train both parents and school staff on how to implement behavioral plans.

Students with HFASD demonstrate a variety of school problems and behaviors that may make it difficult for them to be successful in the classroom. Teachers can be of great help to these students when they recognize that these problems and behaviors are part of the student's unique profile. Even more importantly, teachers can make school a successful experience for students with HFASD when they work proactively in conjunction with parents and other professionals to put strategies in place that will address the issues of these students and increase the possibilities of reaching their true potential.

As we deal with difficult behaviors of students with HFASD, it is worth taking another look at their strengths. We mentioned earlier that students with HFASD typically have many strengths—a passion for learning and a desire to share their knowledge; a large fund of information and an ability to recall that information; strong reading decoding; and a strong vocabulary. In addition, students with HFASD typically have many admirable character traits. When asked to describe their best qualities, responses from kids with HFASD included the following: trustworthy, honest, kind, persistent, power of conviction, and logical (Price & Fisher, 2010). We think that their teachers and parents would agree with this list. When we focus on and promote these strengths and positive character traits, we will encounter fewer behavioral problems.

In the next chapter, we will discuss the range of school options that might appropriately serve students with HFASD and look at how parents can effectively access these services and programs.

chapter 7

Working With the School System

Options for Students With HFASD

As we enter the Model Asperger's Program of the Ivymount School in Potomac, MD, the students have been participating in a cooperative game that requires listening to one another and taking turns. The activity is led by the school's psychologist and speech pathologist and is part of a regularly scheduled daily time that is devoted to developing social skills. The teacher and two instructional assistants also are present in the room. John has become very agitated, because he feels that he did not get a chance to do what he wanted in the game. In return, Sam has become irritated with John's behavior. The other four fifth and sixth graders also seem agitated, as we hear more audible groans and two of the students begin flapping their hands. The adults direct the students to return to their seats. Everyone goes back to his or her desk and the speech-language pathologist begins to lead a discussion about two good things that happened during the group time and two problematic things that happened.

On each student's desk is an individual daily schedule with a behavioral chart incorporated into it. There is also a large visual schedule in the front of the room. Students are carefully prepared for any changes in the schedule. Both the student and teacher rates each of the behaviors listed on the student's individual contract. If the student's assessment of his or her behavior matches that of the teacher, he or she will get extra match points. Points are turned in for rewards. Each student also has two individual goal areas and a self-monitoring chart on his or her desk. It is color coded from green, meaning "smooth ride;" to yellow, meaning "experiencing some turbulence;" to red, meaning "meteor shower." Velcro holds the star that indicates where the student is on scale with each behavior during the class. If the student is moving to yellow or red on his chart, then he is expected to use his individualized strategies to move back to green.

The students talk about how they might handle things differently in the next group time, referring to the visual strategies "to get you back on green" that are posted on the board. They also refer to the posted list of things that they can do to help another student who is having problems. Sam is still very upset and calling out, and as a result, he is quietly directed to go to the time-out room with the psychologist to have some quiet, calming time and then to discuss the incident. John requests and is allowed to go to the alternative area, which is called the space station. He puts on a body sock, referred to as the space suit, to help him calm down. After about 4 minutes, he returns to the group, appearing to be very much under control. As the discussion ends, students are given some down time before the next activity—a social studies lesson involving a written language assignment—will begin. During this down time, one student relaxes on a comfortable chair, two students play games on their laptops, and one searches for information on the Internet.

The class moves into social studies. They are talking about writing historical fiction to tell a story that has to do with the period of history that they have been studying. This is a way of relating an area of interest (in this case, the Lascaux caves in France) to having them write a story, a skill that is a weak area for all of them. The teacher has the tasks of the writing assignment broken down per day, so that the students know what part of the assignment they have to complete each day in order to finish by the end of the week. Everything is spelled out very thoroughly. One of the students is very resistant to writing the historical fiction and is groaning loudly. She is able to tell the teacher that she doesn't want to do it. The teacher tells her that if she comes in tomorrow with another proposal, she will listen to it.

It's now time to begin preparing to go home. Toby is upset when he looks at the schedule of the day and sees that they didn't do one of their scheduled activities. The teacher explains that she was out of the room for a while unexpectedly today and they didn't get to it. She summarizes that sometimes things happen and we have to be flexible. That seems OK with Toby, but the teacher has another child to deal with. Sam is upset that he has a lot of points saved up from good behavior on his contract, and he wants to buy things now, but the teacher reminds him that they buy things at lunchtime. She calmly repeats that the rule is that they can only buy things at lunchtime. She takes the time patiently to go over the rules again. He continues to insist that he wants to buy something now and that he didn't get the opportunity to do so at lunchtime. The teacher helps him understand what he might do next time, if he sees that he's not getting a chance to buy his reward during lunch. After listening calmly to him, she is able to redirect Sam to go back to his desk to pack up to go home.

Ivymount's Model Asperger's Program is an example of one exemplary program that provides services for students with HFASD. Students in this program require the intensive and integrated social and executive skill training that is provided by

Ivymount's expert staff throughout the day. Their needs cannot be adequately met in their neighborhood public schools and they must travel, in some cases long distances, and be separated from their neurotypical peers, to take part in a program that meets their needs. Like students with other disabilities, each case of a student with HFASD must be evaluated individually in order for a determination to be made of what the least restrictive educational environment for that student should be. Each school district should have a continuum of services, ranging from educating students in their neighborhood school with appropriate special education instruction and accommodations available in the regular classroom; to special classes for all or part of the day in a neighborhood school; to a special program located in a public school in the district, other than the neighborhood school; to a special program, in a separate building, serving only students with disabilities, such as Ivymount.

When a parent or teacher suspects that a student has a disability such as ASD that is impacting her educational progress, they have a responsibility to ask that a school meeting be convened to discuss the student and to plan for appropriate interventions. These meetings will generally begin in the form of a parent-teacher conference and then move to a schoolwide child study team and finally to a 504 or IEP meeting if typical school interventions are not enough to make a difference for the student. However, is very important to note that parents can begin the IEP/504 process at any point by writing a letter to the school principal saying that they suspect that their child has an educational disability and is in need of an IEP in order to have a Free Appropriate Public Education (FAPE).

The Road Map in Figure 6 gives parents and teachers a visual map of the path they should follow to get appropriate services for a student who has HFASD and is struggling in school. For some students, the parent conference or child study team recommendations may be enough to provide the interventions that are necessary for the student with HFASD to be successful. For oth-

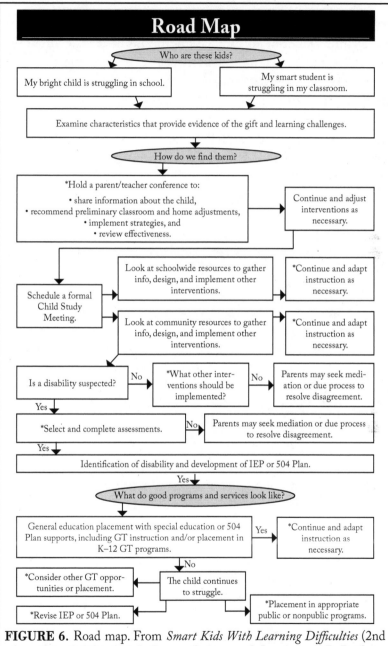

FIGURE 6. Road map. From *Smart Kids With Learning Difficulties* (2nd ed., p. 8) by R. Weinfeld, L. Barnes-Robinson, S. Jeweler, and B. Roffman Shevitz, 2013, Waco, TX: Prufrock Press. Copyright 2013 by Prufrock Press. Reprinted with permission.

ers, a formalized 504 plan will communicate to all staff the need for accommodations in the classroom and in testing situations. For still others, an IEP will be necessary to provide the direct special education instruction and/or school placement that will allow the student to achieve, while minimizing the impact of his or her disability. In our experience, most students with HFASD are best served with an IEP because of the multiplicity and severity of their needs. They require the specialized instruction that typically only comes with an IEP.

Appropriate Teachers and Classrooms for Students With HFASD

Before we discuss the different types of formal plans available to students with HFASD, there are some characteristics that any classroom should have, if students with HFASD are to be successful. As described in the book *Unstuck and On Target!* (Cannon et al., 2011), the classroom should be flexible and supportive. Characteristics of this type of classroom include (Cannon et al., 2011):

» smooth and calm transitions;
» absence of power struggles;
» high ratio of praise to corrections;
» extensive use of active priming/preparation;
» clear, explicit, specific explanations;
» clear routines;
» materials organized; and
» the use of consistent language from staff, such as "open mind, plan A and plan B, and compromise" (p. 9).

Cannon et al. (2011) also described the "flexible and supportive teacher" as someone who:

» has a calm demeanor, empathic understanding, positive outlook, and high expectations;

» problem solves with students to determine the cause of breakdowns;

» knows themselves and how to proactively avoid his or her own inflexibility;

» lives aloud, modeling their own situations requiring flexibility;

» partners with students by empowering them to make choices;

» provides multiple opportunities to practice skills; and

» provides fading, cueing to gradually build skills and independence. (p. 10)

Hans Asperger, who first identified these students, had something to say about the kind of teacher that they needed:

These children often show a surprising sensitivity to the personality of the teacher. They can be taught, but only by those who give them true understanding and affection, people who show kindness towards them and yes, humor. The teacher's underlying attitude influences, involuntarily and unconsciously, the mood and behavior of the child. (Gerhardt, 2012)

As we previously describe in Chapter 5, emphasis should also be placed on teaching to the child's strengths. Teachers who emphasize strengths will need to differentiate in order to focus on each student's individual gifts and interests and learning styles. These teachers will also understand that they can teach rigorous lessons that keep the same high standards they hold for other smart students, while providing for alternative ways to learn and to demonstrate understanding.

Outstanding teachers of these students will teach rigorous lessons that build from the specific to the general. They will make the relevance of the curriculum clear at every opportunity. They will break concepts down into their component parts. They will define all new vocabulary. They will employ a multisensory approach to accommodate the need for visual and tactile reinforcement for some students and the need for verbal reinforcement for others.

Advocating for Appropriate Services

As parents and teachers advocate for appropriate service for students with HFASD, it is crucial that they are aware of the laws and policies that will affect the decision making regarding those services. Below, we will describe some of the key terminology and issues, including the decision of a 504 plan versus an IEP, the definition of Least Restrictive Environment (LRE), the definition of the disability codes that are most likely to be discussed, and the definition of educational impact.

In our experience, it is extremely helpful if parents and at least one school staff member are allied in their beliefs regarding the appropriate services that are needed for the student. It is especially important that parents try to reach a common understanding of what is needed with their ally on the school staff before heading into the formal 504 or IEP meeting. At times, one team member may dominate the formal meeting; therefore, it may be difficult for other parties to speak up. Knowing that there is a school staff person who shares their views often can make all the difference in parents being able to effectively communicate about what is needed for their child.

Having an outside educational consultant or attorney accompany the parents to the school meeting also can be very beneficial. This outside expert will have reviewed all of the child's records, observed the child in the school setting, and spoken informally with both parents and school staff about the student's strengths and needs. Having such a person by their side allows the parents to simply be parents, focusing on their own feelings and beliefs that have led them to this meeting, while the expert can focus on the laws, policies, and dynamics of the decision making. The expert's combined knowledge of what should happen in the meeting, the best practices and methodologies for educating students with HFASD, and his or her knowledge of the individual student, may help make a persuasive case for providing the needed services. It has been our experience that the most effective advocates are those who are knowledgeable and persistent, rather that aggressive and confrontational. The overall goal should be to set a positive climate where everyone will be interested in collaborating in the student's best interest.

504 Versus IEP

Students with HFASD may qualify for a 504 plan or an IEP. Although these are both formal, legal documents that support students with disabilities, there are important differences between the two types of plans. When it is determined that a student has a disability such as HFASD, a 504 team or an IEP team can then determine whether or not the student qualifies for services under that plan. A 504 plan typically provides only for accommodations. Accommodations for a student with HFASD might include many of the suggestions in Chapters 5 and 6 of this book. An IEP could include many of the same accommodations, but would also include specific measurable goals that special educators and other school providers of related service, like speech-language pathologists, occupational therapists, and counselors, would work on with the student over the coming year. Typically, an IEP provides for direct instruction by the special educator. For a student with HFASD, that direct instruction could be focused on helping the student to improve in any of the areas that are affected by his or her disability. For example, the student might have instruction in improving social skills, flexibility, pragmatic language skills, attention skills, organization skills, and/or written language skills. An IEP could result in the student being in a special class for part or all of the day, as well as the possibility that a student could be placed in a special program or school. In determining whether a student qualifies for an IEP, the team considers whether or not there is educational impact related to the student's disability and whether or not she needs specially designed instruction to address that impact. In determining whether a student qualifies for a 504 plan, a school team typically looks at whether learning is affected to the point that the student cannot perform as well as the average student. School teams are often more willing to agree to a 504 plan than an IEP, because a 504 plan typically does not require the provision of staff time or resources.

In order to qualify for a 504 plan, a student must have a disability that significantly limits one or more life functions. For the purposes of school, this life function may be in the area of learning, thinking, communicating, or concentrating, among other areas. Beginning in 2009, the determination of qualification for a 504 plan must consider the ameliorating effects of any mitigating measures that the student is using. For example, a student with HFASD may be receiving support for learned behavioral modifications, or private speech and language services, or tutoring, or social skills training. The 504 team is now directed to consider what the student's performance would be without these supports. In determining whether or not a student qualifies for a 504 plan, the team must go beyond just looking at grades and tests and consider other case-by-case data, such as input from the teachers and parents about how the student is adapting to the school environment.

It is important to say that there has been clear recent guidance from the federal government that no student is too bright to qualify for a 504 plan or IEP, that students are entitled to their 504 plan or IEP accommodations in challenging classes such as honors or Advanced Placement classes, and that students cannot be excluded from these challenging classes because they receive 504 accommodations or special education services (Monroe, 2007).

The IEP

Determination of a Disability for Students With HFASD

When a parent or teacher suspects a disability in a child that may require special education services, an Individualized Education Program meeting should be requested in writing to the school administrator. The first IEP meeting, typically referred to as a screening IEP meeting, will look at the student's educational history, a classroom observation, and a teacher report, along with a report from the parents. The IEP team, typically consisting of a school administrator, a special educator, the child's classroom teacher, the parents, and other school experts such as a school psychologist and/or a speech pathologist, together will discuss the data and attempt to reach consensus about whether or not a disability is suspected. If a disability is suspected, a plan for evaluation will be developed and a second IEP meeting will be scheduled to review the evaluation, make a determination about whether a disability exists, and determine whether an IEP should be developed for the student. The evaluation itself should include a review of any private evaluations that the parents may want to submit, as well as those that will be completed by appropriate school personnel, including the school psychologist and special educator, in all areas of suspected disability. The timeline for holding the second IEP meeting is typically within 60 days of the date that the parents authorize that the evaluation process go forward.

Response to Intervention (RtI) was introduced into the special education law in 2004 as part of the process for identifying students for a possible learning disability. RtI was identified as a way to provide evidence-based instruction to students and frequent assessment of the effectiveness of those interventions. Many school districts have incorporated RtI not only into the process for identifying learning disabilities, but also into the process for considering other disabilities, as well. For students with HFASD, the school team may suggest trying some new interventions and seeing how the student responds to them before identifying the student with a disability. It is important to know that RtI may not be used as a way to delay identification of a student as being eligible for an IEP. Although we welcome employing evidence-based interventions and assessing their effectiveness, once a student is suspected of having a disability, there are timelines that must be followed in determining whether the student is eligible for an IEP.

Students with HFASD typically would be considered for a disability code of autism. However, the student could be considered for any of the 14 federal educational disability codes. Below are the definitions of the most likely codes for which a student with HFASD might be considered. These disability code definitions are taken from the Individuals with Disabilities Education Act (IDEA) revisions of 2006.

Coding for Autism Spectrum Disorder. The most likely, and generally the most accurate, educational disability coding for a student with HFASD is the code for autism. Parents may want to submit reports from a private psychologist, psychiatrist, and/or pediatrician to help the school in its determination of the presence of this disability. The definition from IDEA (2006) is as follows:

> (1)(i) Autism means a developmental disability significantly affecting verbal and nonverbal communication and social interaction, generally evident before age three that adversely affects a child's educational performance. Other characteristics often associated with autism are engagement in repetitive activities and stereotyped movements,

resistance to environmental change or change in daily routines, and unusual responses to sensory experiences.

(ii) Autism does not apply if a child's educational performance is adversely affected, primarily, because the child has an emotional disturbance, as defined in paragraph (c)(4) of this section.

A child who manifests the characteristics of autism after age three could be identified as having autism if the criteria in paragraph (c)(1)(i) of this section are satisfied. (p. 218)

Coding as Speech or Language Impaired. As discussed earlier in this book, students with HFASD frequently have difficulties with pragmatic language, the ability to communicate effectively with others. This language impairment may have a great effect on them in the educational setting. Although most students with HFASD will need goals and services targeted at improving their communication skills, we believe that if they meet the DSM criteria for ASD, then it is more appropriate to identify these students as being on the autism spectrum, in order to give staff a complete understanding of their issues. However, with the new DSM category of Social Communication Disorder (SCD), some students who were previously diagnosed as being on the autistic spectrum, as a result of their diagnoses of Asperger's syndrome or PDD-NOS, may now be diagnosed as having SCD. It is important to recognize that if the child has or previously had repetitive or rigid behaviors and sensory problems in addition to having social problems then she qualifies for an ASD diagnosis, not an SCD diagnosis. Many students who were previously diagnosed as having Nonverbal Learning Disorder may also now qualify for a diagnosis of SCD. We believe that some IEP teams will classify students who have been identified with SCD as having a speech and language impairment. This change brings with it some concerns. There is a national shortage of speech-language pathologists, and there may be resistance to identifying more students who will need their services. There also is concern that, while we would welcome the expertise of speech-language pathologists who are experienced in providing services to improve pragmatic language and nonverbal communication, many school speech-language pathologists are only experienced in working on articulation, expressive, and receptive language. It will also be very important that we advocate for students with SCD who qualify for IEPs based on their identification as having a speech and language impairment to have IEPs with goals, accommodations, and services in all areas that are affected by their disability. For many, this will go beyond speech and language and may involve areas such as written expression, reading comprehension, organization, and attention, as well as social understanding and social skills.

Speech and language impairment is defined in IDEA (2006) as follows:

> Speech or language impairment means a communication disorder, such as stuttering, impaired articulation, a language impairment, or a voice impairment, that adversely affects a child's educational performance. (p. 219)

Coding for Emotional Disturbance. There are times that the concern that is presenting itself to the school team is mainly behavioral. The school team, including parents, may be unaware that the student has a diagnosis of ASD or may feel that this condition is secondary to his emotional problems. But the fact is that the core deficits in ASD, which are poor social understanding and brain-based inflexibility, do not arise secondary to emotional problems, while the reverse is often true. When deficits in social understanding and flexibility are not addressed at school, students can become isolated, anxious, and even depressed. We do want to caution parents and school staff that what may appear to be emotional disturbance may, in fact, be a result of the frustration, anxiety, and/or depression the student is experiencing as a result of her needs related to ASD not being met. Parents and school staff should be further cautioned that placement of children with HFASD in a class of students with emotional disturbance may be a serious mismatch of educational and instructional goals, accommodations, and services. Emotional disturbance is defined in IDEA (2006) as follows:

(4)(i) Emotional disturbance means a condition exhibiting one or more of the following characteristics over a long period of time and to a marked degree that adversely affects a child's educational performance:

(a) An inability to learn that cannot be explained by intellectual, sensory, or health factors.

(b) An inability to build or maintain satisfactory interpersonal relationships with peers and teachers.

(c) Inappropriate types of behavior or feelings under normal circumstances.

(d) A general pervasive mood of unhappiness or depression.

(e) A tendency to develop physical symptoms or fears associated with personal or school problems.

(ii) Emotional disturbance includes schizophrenia. The term does not apply to children who are socially maladjusted, unless it is determined that they have an emotional disturbance under paragraph (c)(4)(i) of this section. (p. 218)

Coding for Other Health Impairment. Students with HFASD may be considered for coding as students who are "other health impaired." This consideration may be appropriate, as the student's educational progress may also be affected by a health condition such as ADHD or Tourette's syndrome. However, once again, in an effort to accurately code students, it is important that effects of the HFASD be evaluated and understood. It may, in fact, be the case that the lack of attention or limited alertness that the student is demonstrating is more related to the mismatch between his needs and the school environment than it is to any other health condition. Other health impairment is defined in IDEA (2006) as follows:

> (9) Other health impairment means having limited strength, vitality, or alertness, including a heightened alertness to environmental stimuli, that results in limited alertness with respect to the educational environment, that—
>
> (i) Is due to chronic or acute health problems such as asthma, attention deficit disorder or attention deficit hyperactivity disorder, diabetes, epilepsy, a heart condition, hemophilia, lead poisoning, leukemia, nephritis, rheumatic fever, sickle cell anemia, and Tourette's syndrome; and
>
> (ii) Adversely affects a child's educational performance. (p. 219)

Coding for a Specific Learning Disability. Staff and parents may see a disparity between the student's cognitive potential as demonstrated by his verbal or spatial abilities, as evident in his area of passion, and his academic weaknesses such as written expression, reading comprehension, and organization. A study by Griswold, Barnhill, Myles, Hagiwara, and Simpson (2002) found that students with Asperger's syndrome had lower achievement scores in written expression, listening comprehension, and numerical operations than the general population. Although students with HFASD may respond to some of the instructional interventions used for students with learning disabilities, a better understanding of their unique constellation of strengths and needs typically comes from accurate coding under the autism classification. Specific learning disabilities are defined in IDEA (2006) as follows:

> Specific Learning Disability—(i) General. Specific learning disability means a disorder in one or more of the basic psychological processes involved in understanding or in using language, spoken or written, that may manifest itself in the imperfect ability to listen, think, speak, read, write, spell, or to do mathematical calculations, including conditions such as perceptual disabilities, brain injury, minimal brain dysfunction, dyslexia, and developmental aphasia.
>
> (ii) Disorders not included. Specific learning disability does not include learning problems that are primarily the result of visual, hearing, or motor disabilities, of mental retardation, of emotional disturbance, or of environmental, cultural, or economic disadvantage. (p. 219)

In summary, students with HFASD may qualify for special education services through their identification as being labeled with any of a variety of educational disability codes. Although we believe that identifying students with the autism coding is generally the most accurate and helpful identification, regardless of which coding is used the student can qualify for all of the appropriate services that he needs. It is the goals and objectives of the IEP, and the accommodations, not the coding, that actually drive the services and placement. The next step toward qualifying for an IEP is to look at whether or not the student's disability impacts his educational progress.

Educational Impact

Once it has been determined that a disability exists, the next step in determining whether or not the student qualifies for an

IEP is the consideration of whether or not the student's disability impacts his education. This is often a very difficult decision and can be somewhat contentious. The parents may see the educational impact in the fact that the student is anxious and depressed, is spending long hours outside of school studying in an effort to keep up, and/or that his or her self-esteem is plummeting. School staff may not see the educational impact, as the student may not display his emotional issues during the school day and his grades may be adequate. How to determine educational impact is not defined in the law and is often the source of disagreement at school meetings. Some school officials have described educational impact as including academic impact, as well as other things that may prevent a child from participating in the life of a classroom. This unofficial definition at least opens the door to look beyond grades and test scores to the student's participation in the entire school day. As advocates for students with HFASD, it is important for parents and teachers to look not only at the data about a student's educational performance, but also to his or her entire experience of the school environment.

A landmark case for students with Asperger's syndrome was the decision in a U.S. District Court in Maine in 2006 (*Mr. and Mrs. I v. Maine School Administrative District No. 55*). The court said that the school district must not define impact too narrowly (just looking at grades and other academic components), but must look at the impact the disability has on social interactions and how this in turn affects social-emotional well-being during the school day.

The Need for Specialized Instruction

Finally, the third question after determining whether the student has a disability and whether there is educational impact is the question of whether or not the student needs specialized instruction to access the curriculum. It is important to remember that special education should be designed to meet the unique needs of a child with a disability and to address the needs that result from that disability. In the case of HFASD, those needs may not necessarily be in reading, writing, or math. The needs may be more in the areas of social communication, and areas of executive functioning such as organization, flexibility, and/or attention.

As most states move into implementation of the Common Core State Standards (CCSS), it will also be necessary to expand our definition of what it means to have access to the curriculum. The CCSS curriculum will not only emphasize achievement in reading, writing, and mathematics, but will also emphasize the learning process, including the ability to work with others and to demonstrate executive functioning issues such as metacognition about one's own learning processes. These learning processes are exactly the areas with which so many students with HFASD have difficulties. We believe that more students with HFASD than ever will need specialized instruction as public school districts transition to the CCSS.

Determination of FAPE

One of the standards for development of an IEP is that each student's plan be calculated to provide a Free and Appropriate Public Education (FAPE). In the past, FAPE has been described as providing a basic "floor of opportunity," and school systems have often argued that they are only required by law to provide programs from which the students derive "some educational benefit" (*Board of Education of Hendrick Hudson Central School District, Westchester City v. Rowley*, 1982, p. 200). An important new court decision expands this definition of FAPE to include the requirement that IEPs should be designed to help the student achieve independence and self-sufficiency. Expanding on this concept, a Washington court ruled in 2006 that specific methodologies need to be included in the IEP and that accommodations alone are not sufficient to meet this need (*J. L., M. L. & K. L. v. Mercer Island School District*). Rather than accommodations alone, specially designed instruction for improving the student's skills must be included in each IEP. This court decision is particularly significant for students with HFASD. The concept that FAPE includes a requirement that IEPs should be aimed at the outcomes of independence and self-sufficiency has been supported in several recent court decisions and may open the door to more targeted and comprehensive services for these students. Improved social skills and executive functioning skills certainly are needed by many students with HFASD if they are to become independent and self-sufficient.

Designing The IEP

Once the decisions have been made that a student has an educational disability and qualifies for an IEP, goals and objectives are designed to address the student's identified needs. Regardless of the coding, goals and objectives should be designed to address all areas that are impacted by the student's disability. These impact areas need to be clearly defined in the present levels of the IEP. Parents and other advocates for students with HFASD should look at the Big 10 (see Chapter 6, pp. 91–145) list for possible impact areas. When reviewing goals, they should be understandable and measurable. They should contain the conditions that should be present for the student to demonstrate proficiency in the goal, the specific observable target behavior that will be measured, the criteria that will show the student has mastered the goal, and the documentation that will show whether or not the goal has been achieved. For example, a student with a need in the area of social interactions might have a goal like this one: "Given social skills instruction, social stories, and suggested questions, the student will participate in a conversation on a topic initiated by another student, for at least five exchanges, as observed in 3 out of 4 formal observations." In addition to goals, supplementary aids and services that need to be present in the classroom, as well as accommodations that are needed in test situations, are included in the IEP. When determining appropriate classroom and testing aids and accommodations, it is important to focus on the strengths of the student. For example, a student with strong visual skills could have the accommodation of creating a web of his ideas, perhaps with the help of computer software, before he begins writing.

Definition of Least Restrictive Environment

Finally, a determination is made regarding where the student will receive the services described in his or her IEP. Federal and state laws mandate that each student's needs be met in the Least Restrictive Environment (LRE). However, it is important to remember that what is the LRE for one student may not meet the needs of another student. On one hand, the law calls for efforts to be made to educate students with their nondisabled peers. On the other hand, the law clearly states that if the "nature or severity of the disability is such that education in regular classes with the use of supplementary aids and services cannot be achieved satisfactorily . . ." children with disabilities may be removed from the regular environment (IDEA, 2006, p. 226–227). The law also clearly states that each public agency must ensure that a continuum of alternative placements is available and that these placements include instruction in regular classes with a resource room or itinerant support, special classes, special schools, home instruction, and instruction in hospitals and institutions. Sometimes school officials will argue that to provide the LRE, a student who is identified as needing special education services must first be served in the regular classroom with supports, and only after this fails can she be considered for a special class or special school placement. We do not believe that this is an accurate interpretation of the law. Instead, we believe that the determination of the LRE is an individual decision regarding what environment is the least restrictive for the student in question for the coming year. This decision, like other IEP decisions, should be reviewed and adjusted on at least a yearly basis, during the mandated annual review. The chart in Figure 7 (Weinfeld & Davis, 2008) shows the range of possible placements from Least Restrictive to Most Restrictive.

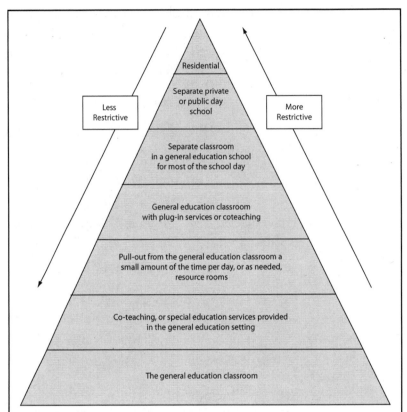

FIGURE 7. A sample placement continuum. From *Special Needs Advocacy Resource Book* (p. 133) by R. Weinfeld and M. Davis, 2008, Waco, TX: Prufrock Press. Copyright 2008 by Prufrock Press. Reprinted with permission.

IDEA defines LRE as follows:

€300.114 LRE requirements.

(2) Each public agency must ensure that—

(i) To the maximum extent appropriate, children with disabilities, including children in public or private institutions or other care facilities, are educated with children who are nondisabled; and

(ii) Special classes, separate schooling, or other removal of children with disabilities from the regular educational environment occurs only if the nature or severity of the disability is such that education in regular classes with the use of supplementary aids and services cannot be achieved satisfactorily.

€300.115 Continuum of alternative placements.

(a) Each public agency must ensure that a continuum of alternative placements is available to meet the needs of children with disabilities for special education and related services.

(b) The continuum required in paragraph (a) of this section must—

(1) Include the alternative placements listed in the definition of special education under €300.38 (instruction in regular classes, special classes, special schools, home instruction, and instruction in hospitals and institutions); and

(2) Make provision for supplementary services (such as resource room or itinerant instruction) to be provided in conjunction with regular class placement. (IDEA, 2006, pp. 226–227)

Program Options

As described in the discussion of LRE above, program options for students with HFASD range from the typical classroom to separate schools, depending on the nature and severity of the student's disability.

Instruction in Regular Classes

Students identified with HFASD may receive all of their education in the regular classroom. General educators, with consultation from special education teachers and service providers, may provide the needed supplementary aids and accommodations and work on helping students to improve in their areas of weakness. Special educators and service providers may visit the classroom to provide services to the students, without having them miss classroom instruction or be segregated from the life of the classroom.

When considering inclusion in a typical classroom, as well as the other options that we will discuss, students can receive a variety of supports. One of the supports that can be considered in any environment is having a paraeducator available to the student for part or all of the school day. A skilled paraeducator can assist the student in a way that is unobtrusive and helps the student to deal with difficult social interactions, while removing the obstacles that are created by any of the other Big 10 issues. Although parents may be eager to advocate for the solution of having a paraeducator, there are pitfalls that should be considered as well. Paraeducators are typically not well paid and don't usually have the expertise and experience of special education teachers or related service providers. In our experience, paraeducators will need a great deal of training and supervision to know how and when to effectively help the student. A paraeducator who provides a student with less than he needs may not be truly effective. A paraeducator who provides a student with more than she needs may create an environment for the child that separates her more than necessary from her nondisabled peers and actually creates an environment that is more restrictive than necessary.

Instruction in Special Classes

In order to provide special education instruction to the student with HFASD, it may be beneficial for the special educator or related service provider (speech-language pathologist, psychologist, counselor, or occupational therapist) to see the student in an individual or small-group session outside of the classroom. This pull-out model allows for specialized instruction to be delivered to the student in an environment where it does not distract others or make the student obviously stand out by having other students observe his special instruction. These special classes are especially important and useful when the instruction that will be provided is different or supplementary to what is being done in the regular class. It also allows for small-group or individual instruction, which may be more beneficial to some students with HFASD. Many students with HFASD benefit from receiving the support of a resource room period that serves as a home base within the school day, where they can receive support with organization, written language, and other academic issues, while also receiving coaching regarding social skills issues.

Special Schools

Some students with HFASD may not benefit from education in regular classes. For them, the potential harmful effects of removing them from their neighborhood school are outweighed by the benefits of receiving appropriate education throughout the day from a highly trained staff that is knowledgeable about HFASD and able to provide an environment that incorporates all of the needed interventions, while integrating services throughout the day. Some students are so challenged by mainstream environments that they become easily overwhelmed. These students may require an element of protective emotional safety that is provided by some separate, special schools. Special schools generally provide a smaller student-to-staff ratio, allowing for greater individualization of specialized instruction.

Alternative School Programs

Some parents may opt to place their children in alternative schools that may or may not be special education schools. These schools may provide an environment for students, with or without disabilities, that is a better match for the strengths and needs of the specific student with HFASD. Parents are cautioned to make sure that the staff has expertise in working with students with HFASD and that the methodology that will be employed is truly a good match for their child. These schools differ from the special schools described above in that they are not necessarily state certified in special education.

Homeschooling

Some parents have opted to take their children out of school environments that they perceive as not helpful or possibly harmful and instead provide education for them at home. We believe that, in general, this should only be done for students with HFASD in extreme situations and then, only until a suitable program can be found. One of the primary needs of students with HFASD is that they work at developing their social skills. There are times when homeschooling is done especially well and can provide the right environment for students with HFASD. Some parents have made the homeschooling environment work for their students by connecting with other homeschoolers to provide regular social activities. There are many homeschooling curricula available for general education, which parents of students with HFASD can augment by providing opportunities for social interaction and other needed supports in the community. We still feel that it is unusual that parents would have sufficient expertise in the best practices of working with students with HFASD to be the best educators for their child over the long run.

Home and Hospital Teaching

There may be times in the life of the student with HFASD when his emotional distress related to his HFASD becomes so severe that it is in his best interest that he be removed from the school environment. At this time, mental health professionals should work with the student while he is receiving home tutoring or participating in a full or partial day hospitalization to stabilize him, with the goal of returning him to his school placement. There are a small percentage of students with HFASD who regularly experience a high level of emotional distress for whom home and hospital teaching or hospitalization is periodically required.

Services Available at Different Points Along the "Road"

In conclusion, although we have been focusing on how students with HFASD may qualify for an IEP and what school services may be provided once they have been identified, it is important to again remember that school services should be provided to a student with HFASD regardless of whether or not he has been formally identified for a 504 plan or IEP. As parents and teachers move through the process identified on the Road Map (see Figure 4, p. 151), there is an opportunity for the interventions outlined in Chapters 5 and 6 to be employed and adjusted. Beginning with the first parent-teacher conference and continuing on through child-study teams, and potentially beyond into formal plans, interventions should be selected, data should be kept on the effectiveness of the interventions, and meetings should be reconvened to look at whether the interventions need to be continued, modified, or replaced with other, possibly more effective, interventions. Students with HFASD will be successful in school when parents and school staff work together to select appropriate interventions, continue to dialogue about their effectiveness, and adjust the interventions, services, and school placement accordingly.

chapter 8

Best Practices for Parenting and Raising Kids With HFASD

At first, there was denial, then anger, then grief, and finally, gradual acceptance. Even now, years later, some days Kara's parents can accept that their child has HFASD and some days they cannot. At first, there was the search for the perfect diagnosis that would explain everything and then provide the magical solution that would cure Kara's problems. Gradually, that was replaced with the understanding that what was important was not so much how her problems or the program where she would go to school were labeled, but whether her education was the right match for her strengths and needs. At first, her parents felt guilt and self-doubt every time there was a new theory regarding a possible cause. Gradually, that was replaced with the acceptance of knowing that an answer to what was truly the cause of Kara's disorder may be in the distant future. At first, there was difficulty finding helpful professionals and trusting them when they told them about the challenges that their child faced. Gradually, that was replaced by a desire to make alliances and to work with and trust the professionals who would go above and beyond to see that Kara received appropriate educational services. At first, Kara's parents felt embarrassed that their child was different, less than perfect, and didn't always fit in with others. Gradually, that was replaced with a focus on and celebration of Kara's strengths and a growing desire to challenge others who could only see their little girl's deficits.

One of the biggest problems that parents experience during the early development of children with disabilities, including HFASD, is confusion over diagnosis. Most parents go to experts for diagnosis and answers about their child. They may obtain the wrong diagnosis or one that is not specific enough. Some experts refuse to use the word autism even when it is clear that the criteria apply and others can be confusing in how they present diagnoses to parents. Because HFASD is generally suspected later in a child's developmental stages, it is often confused with many other conditions. And, because the American Psychiatric Association's DSM system did not feature HFASD, particularly Asperger's syndrome, until 1994, the diagnosis was not fully adopted into practice in the professional community until relatively recent times. Still, there is considerable confusion, lack of experience, and lack of standards surrounding the diagnosis of ASD (Lord et al., 2012). This is one reason that Asperger's syndrome as a separate diagnosis has been eliminated in the new DSM-5 and subsumed under the more inclusive category of autism spectrum disorder referred to here as ASD. It is difficult generating accurate expectations when the diagnosis is not clear. A clear diagnosis permits a fuller understanding of the challenges and potential of a child. It is also essential for building the right school and private treatment plan. So getting an accurate, clearly explained diagnosis is an essential first step in providing a child with what is needed to reach his full potential.

When HFASD information crystallizes and the diagnostic picture clarifies, there is often a period of bereavement when the child is not what parents expected. Often, you must protect yourself to deal with the shock of feeling that your child is "different." This might involve various forms of defensiveness and, frequently, an initial period of denial. There are also problems dealing with public embarrassment when the child is atypical in behavior. There may be the experience of early school rejection, either of being asked to leave a program or not getting admitted to the school you desired for your child.

Problems of speech and language and clumsiness generally are observed first. Before the classification is clear, you might hear a diagnosis of "multisystem disorder," "multihandicapped," "multidisabled," or "developmental delay." Although these general terms are cautious, they often are not made more specific, and these vague labels can last into adolescence without clarity. Psychologists and educators often find themselves reassessing children to clarify the diagnosis along the way.

When facing the stress of dealing with the facts of a child's disability, parents need to be on the same team with each other. They need to discuss their expectations and philosophy of child rearing openly with each other. It is important to try to have complementary and consistent parenting styles. Parents should avoid giving mixed messages whenever possible. This requires ongoing marital communication. Rearing a child with disabilities can be stressful to any marriage. The couple rarely seems to have time to take a vacation alone, and many never have a weekend away or even a date for years. Obtaining good respite care is important to allow parents time alone together. Clinical experience and research reflect parents' feelings of guilt when they understandably lose patience with their child with disabilities (Little, 2002). Parents must protect themselves and each other from guilt and stress. Getting adequate rest and recreation is part of that formula.

Parents also need to be a team when dealing with the school system. They shouldn't give the school conflicting messages and expectations, argue in front of IEP teams, or create confusion by contacting several different people in the school at once. Sometimes an educational advocate may be useful in working with a school system that might appear to be putting up barriers to services and supports. See Chapter 4 for more on the development of a team in an action plan.

Look back at the Big 10 issues discussed in Chapter 6 (see pp. 91–145). These are all areas where intervention may be needed to support your child. We'll discuss ways you can address some of these areas and other issues that appear in the home life of a child with HFASD in the sections that follow.

Handling Social Skills Deficits

Because social skill deficits are at the core of HFASD, it is understandable that one might experience frustration in helping a child initiate and maintain friendships and avoid peer rejection. Social clubs and interest groups that match a child's areas of expertise and passion can be helpful. Some therapeutic and recreational afterschool groups are geared to include children with special needs. Children with HFASD also can act as tutors in the community in areas of their special academic strengths. Social skill therapy groups frequently are geared specifically for children with HFASD. Much repetition of specific skills may be required. This may involve direct instruction on theory of mind, reading faces, interpreting gestures, and rehearsing and practice of social routines. Much daily learning experience can be embedded in a social context of interaction and sharing throughout the day in and out of school. Parents can be a child's most powerful coach by actively and explicitly decoding what body language they see in another family member or movie character that gives hints about what the person might be thinking or feeling. They can also talk out loud about what might be motivating a person to act as they are and what they might do next. This type of decoding can be very powerful for a child with HFASD who does not automatically draw meaning from the social cues of others, or even realize that he needs to pay attention to them in order to understand what is going on. Many approaches to social skills deficits have been addressed throughout this book, and specific methods for improving social skills can be found in Chapter 6.

Teaching Manners

Many children with HFASD fail to practice good private hygiene behavior. Nose picking, failing to comb hair, and other unhygienic behaviors are not uncommon. Hygiene skills must be directly taught and maintained. Fortunately, these are rule-governed behaviors, which can be memorized. A website called Teacher Planet has a wide range of resources on etiquette for children (visit http://www.teacherplanet.com/resource/manners.php). Some of these resources include visual posters that can be mounted on a wall and used to reinforce good manners. In some areas, consultants are available to teach manners through direct instruction. For example, a class could be taught to model a formal dinner party using proper etiquette, a scenario that would introduce multiple social skills rules to a child with HFASD without singling him out for his poor manners. A class on restaurant manners can culminate in a visit to a restaurant.

At home, parents also can outline and review general rules for good hygiene behavior and manners. They should model what is private hygiene and what is public hygiene behavior (such as covering one's mouth when coughing). Checklists, rewards, and other consequences programs also can be implemented to teach these skills.

Dealing With Problems With Flexibility and Organization

Children with HFASD usually have problems with flexibility and organization (Hill, 2004; Kenworthy et al., 2009) that make it hard to shift from one activity to another, accommodate unexpected events, accept conflicting viewpoints, and carry out basic routines, like getting ready for school and bringing home and turning in their homework (see Chapter 3). These problems are hard on parents, who often end up having to provide much more direct support and guidance than is typically required. The good news is that parents can directly teach flexibility and organization skills by modeling the use of scripts and routines that help children with HFASD handle the unexpected, avoid getting stuck, and complete multistep tasks. *Unstuck and On Target Everywhere: Teaching Executive Functions in Everyday Life* (Kenworthy et al., 2014) gives specific suggestions about how to help a child with HFASD learn to be more flexible and goal directed. *Superflex: A Social Thinking Curriculum* (Madrigal & Winner, 2008) also targets flexibility and behavior regulation.

Managing Attention

Attention problems are among the most common coexisting conditions in HFASD (estimates indicate that approximately one third of children with HFASD have full-blown ADHD as well; Leyfer et al., 2006). The key features of ADHD are impulsivity, motor restlessness, and inattention. Generally, ADHD is a problem of restraint, inhibition, and self-modulation. It is about sustaining effort and motivation as much as it is about attention problems. At this point, the research on the topic is voluminous. What is clear from research, especially from a massive, groundbreaking NIMH study (Jensen, Hinshaw, & Swanson, 2001), is that ADHD should be treated with multiple approaches or a multimodal approach. Silverman, Iseman, and Jeweler (2009) have proposed a wraparound plan for managing ADHD. We also direct readers to the work of Drs. Russell Barkley, Keith Connors, Sam Goldstein, and Kathleen Nadeau for good explanations of the diagnosis, treatment, behavior management, and education of students with ADHD.

Attention problems may be revealed by a single symptom or multiple ones. A short attention span, limited endurance, effortfulness, and executive functioning problems are often found in children with autism. ADHD may be a full-blown coexisting condition, or some symptoms may be a part of the autism symptomotology. For example, absorption in self (the original meaning of the term "autism") due to lack of reciprocity skills, fixation on objects and ideas, and self-stimulatory behaviors can divert attention in autism, creating a different source of attention problems than that seen in ADHD without autism. Also, when we think of persons with ADHD, we often think that they operate quickly in all things, thinking of the hyperactive or impulsive types. Actually, persons with solely inattentive forms of ADHD (without hyperactivity) and autism may display very slow processing skills in some areas.

If parents suspect that their child with HFASD may also struggle with focusing attention, inhibiting impulses (or "putting the brakes on"), or keeping their bodies still and mouths quiet, they should pursue the following multimodal plan for identifying, and if necessary, treating, attention deficits with or without hyperactivity (adapted from Silverman et al., 2009).

1. Accurate assessment of the ADHD symptoms should be conducted, including medical, neurological, psychiatric, psychological, neuropsychological, social, family systems, educational, and other evaluations as needed. Medical conditions such as thyroid dysfunction and allergies should be ruled out.

2. The child's strengths should be identified. It is very important to approach ADHD with a strengths model,

because 50%–70% of children with ADHD display negative behaviors that can be irritating to parents and teachers. The view of the child with ADHD needs to be "reframed" conceptually in a positive manner. This strengths-based model is effective, because it is the child's strengths that eventually carry his self-esteem and self-concept forward. Regardless of disability, a strengths approach is important.

3. Parent education should be provided in an intervention plan, including books, films, lecture series, seminars, parent training programs, and association membership. For example, a wide variety of materials, activities, and other supports may be found by consulting the organization called Children and Adults with Attention Deficit Disorders (CHADD). Parent training should include direct instruction in behavior management. Parents can also help to enhance executive functioning.

4. Parent counseling regarding child management may be required with checkups as needed. An attempt should be made to maximize consistency between significant adults in the child's life in philosophy and techniques of child rearing. Parenting stress should be kept in mind and addressed. Consultation is also suggested with a behavior specialist who can educate parents in basic techniques, such as reinforcement systems (e.g., sticker charts and rewards for desired behaviors, countdown procedures for warning children to stop/start a behavior, ignoring strategies, etc.)

5. If the child receives an ADHD diagnosis, then a treatment plan should be developed which includes consideration of pharmacological interventions. Medications and positive behavior management techniques are the two best-studied and most proven treatments for ADHD. Consultation with a physician who is a specialist in children and developmental disorders regarding medication

options can educate parents about and the costs and benefits of medication.

6. Case management is assigned to someone (e.g., therapist, school counselor, special educator, school nurse), who communicates with all relevant parties regarding medications and preplanned intervention strategies. Parents frequently contact several school officials at once. It is more effective for all involved to have one pivotal person in the school to maintain ongoing contact.

7. A 504 plan may be developed with accommodations. Special education coding as "other health impaired" may be established through special education eligibility meetings in addition to the autism coding under federal law (see the discussion of coding, IEPs, and 504 plans in Chapter 7). If possible, the child should be coached to attend these meetings and to take ownership of the main objectives. Keep the number of objectives prioritized, few, and simple. The "Other Health Impaired Code" would be second in priority to the "autism" special education classification. Some school systems only permit one key classification in their data systems, so the primary special education classification should be "autism."

8. A school/home contract is used to monitor schoolwork and homework. A school class-by-class monitoring sheet may be necessary with home reinforcements for good behavior. Class work, homework, and organizational skill objectives may be identified as requirements for each subject. Monitor effectiveness of strategies through periodic teacher and parent ratings of attention, activity level, and related personality/behavior variables. Children may be rewarded at home for positive school ratings. Keep the number of objectives down, from three to five at a time.

9. Environmental stress factors are assessed. Stressors at school and home should be identified. Family stress

reduction activities are selected and employed by parents, including respite opportunities and vacations.

10. Individual and/or group counseling for the child focuses on self-evaluation, self-monitoring, educational self-advocacy, and social skills. Peer relations and self-esteem issues are addressed. This is important because of the high rates of peer rejection experienced by children with ADHD, autism, and other differences.

11. The child's diet is reviewed for basic good nutrition.

12. Calming and relaxation techniques are explored. These practices include yoga, meditation, and relaxation therapies. Although they may not be curative in themselves, they can be helpful to an overall treatment plan. The child needs to learn what being calm feels like as a base experience.

13. Teacher support is provided regarding management, class environment factors, accommodations, and teaching techniques appropriate for the child. An FBA and behavior plan may be required.

Dealing With Oppositional Behavior

Rigidity is typically hardwired into the brains of children with HFASD. Rigidity can lead to oppositional resistance under stress. Opposition can be avoided by careful anticipation of likely stressors, having accurate expectations of how stressors will be addressed, and through planning to ignore or respond more flexibly to the situation when it arises. Rigidity and stubbornness are not necessarily active choices that your child is making. Many children are seen to "lock up" and become oppositional or defiant when faced with stress. Locking up is a way of handling the feeling of being overwhelmed, which stems from the complexity of information or demands for responses your child is experiencing. It is best to provide time for release of the emotion and the frustration that leads to oppositional behavior and the provision of positive consequences for more effective behaviors. Intelligent ignoring, or choosing not to react to negative provocation, and avoiding power struggles always are important and effective tools to use in dealing with opposition. When possible, positive alternative behavior choices should be introduced and reinforced. It generally does not work to engage in an oppositional, confrontational struggle. Whenever possible, irrational provocation is best dealt with through redirection or by the presentation of "win-win" strategies or choices after the child is calm enough to consider them.

Sometimes a behavior analyst can be brought in as a consultant to decrease more persistent oppositional behaviors.

Dealing With Obsessions

Obsessive interests are a key aspect of HFASD, and to many, they seem to represent a cognitive strength in children with HFASD. Obsessive preoccupations can, however, interfere with learning other things. Sometimes collections of things or ideas are systemized but not practical. Children with HFASD can be rewarded with time to spend in their area of special interest, as well as materials to use, as a condition of completing assigned, but less desirable, tasks such as homework problems. Their obsessions can also be socially embedded or used in a required social chain of events, such as table games that require taking turns. Special interests can also be the way a child with HFASD makes friends, through clubs or other organized activities that involve the special interest. Vocationally, with some effort, a person with HFASD can be encouraged to find work that involves her interests in some practical manner. Strategies for utilizing the areas of interest are offered in Chapter 6.

We should not discount a child's obsession because it is a way that the child finds comfort through organizing the world, but we should monitor to make sure that time spent on the interest is not preventing the child from engaging in important activities such as social interactions and school work. Clear rules and boundaries should be described and enforced to the child as to when she can pursue her obsessions. For example, a parent can set the rule that the child may not work on classifying her latest bug collection specimens during her grandmother's weekly Saturday afternoon visits, but she may be allowed an hour to work independently and without interruption on her interest after grandma has left, if she displayed proper behavior (also pre-set by the parent) during the visit. Take caution, however, that children with HFASD depend on predictable, scheduled, routine situations, and any planned rules pursuing obsessive interests must be adhered to by the parents. In the above example, if Grandma is sick and cannot visit, the parent should discuss the change in routine with the child and set a new rule (i.e., if the child helps the parent with the household chores during the time that Grandma usually visits, she will still be able to have her quiet time to work on her bug collection).

Dealing With Sensory Sensitivities

Sensory sensitivities are part of the new diagnostic criteria for ASD and are very common. Children with HFASD are frequently comfortable hugging a parent but few others. This is to be expected. If tactile irritability is present in a child, it is not generally helpful to force physical contact. It is interesting to note that many children with HFASDs appear to respond better to deep pressure, such as that used in massage or compression, than they do to more typical, lighter touch. This is an area where it is often best to accommodate the child when possible rather than trying to fight or modulate their nervous systems. For example, if he doesn't like wool clothing, then it is easier to find an alternative than to try to treat the problem. There are other areas of sensory sensitivity that must be addressed such as lighting, noises, and food textures. It is very difficult to try to desensitize children to the effect that such environmental factors have on the child. If it is possible to accommodate for the oversensitivity, then that is generally easier than trying to have the child learn to avoid or ignore the issues. Some situations, such as institutional lighting, the sound of heating fans and compressors turning on and off, etc., cannot be avoided. It is also impossible to modulate the sound of thunder or the intensity of public safety alarms.

Dealing With Anxiety

Anxiety is also a frequent coexisting condition in children with HFASD (Leyfer et al., 2006). There are several forms of anxiety that parents may observe in their children. One form of anxiety is generalized (i.e., the child is anxious about many things and in many situations) and chronic, which is more hard-wired as a coexisting condition. Evidence-based treatments for this form of anxiety in autism include Cognitive Behavioral Therapy that targets awareness of symptoms, developing coping strategies, and exposure techniques (Dawson & Burner, 2011). Medication as prescribed by a physician who specializes in children with developmental disorders may also be helpful. Social anxiety is part of the fundamental picture of HFASD, because social coping skills are lacking. Social anxiety responds to a wide range of coordinated cognitive behavioral treatments, which include direct instruction, and techniques such as social stories, scripts, and role-playing. Anxiety also arises when there is the experience or anticipation of being overwhelmed by too much information, novelty, or complexity. This can happen in the instructional setting in classrooms, the cafeteria, hallways of schools, at the beach, in a mall, or anywhere there is a wide range of intense and unpredictable stimuli or demands. Changing or avoiding stressful environments, as well as specific preparation and rehearsal of acquired coping mechanisms, may be required. Sometimes a parent or teacher can promise that a "surprise" is coming in advance, so that children can be prepared for uncertainty. There are also specific stressors that can be addressed through anxiety. One book that addresses these approaches is *Anxiety-Free Kids: An Interactive Guide for Parents and Children* (Zucker, 2008).

One of the most challenging forms of anxiety is spiraling anxiety, where the child feels out of control in any of the situations mentioned above. Providing a calming place or activity to help the child gain control of his or her anxiety is a necessity. Some examples of such activities are included in Chapter 6. A simple meditation technique also might be helpful in stabilizing and recentering your child. Many children don't know what it feels like to be calm and at peace. For them, this experience is new and must be learned through a self-modulating experience such as meditation or relaxation therapy. A treatment plan is more thoroughly presented in Chapter 4.

Expressing and Reciprocating Affection

Children with HFASD frequently feel affection but do not know how to appropriately express these feelings. They need to have guidelines as to who is an appropriate recipient of affection and under which conditions. They need to know when someone is a friend or an acquaintance and when intimacy is appropriate.

The first step in reciprocity is simply looking in the direction of the person with whom one is conversing. It is not necessary to look into the other person's eyes in a locked manner at all times. Making eye contact has many cultural variations and implications. Although it is expected in many Western societies, in other cultures, eye contact has different meanings. For example, in some parts of Asia, the eyes are considered to be the "windows of the soul." There, anger and sexual impulses are believed to be transmitted by staring directly into the eyes. Therefore, direct eye contact, especially between the sexes, is often frowned upon. We suggest that the recipient of eye contact is generally satisfied if the person with whom he or she is conversing looks in the direction of the recipient's face. Many educators and therapists insist on strong eye contact, but this may be culturally insensitive in some cases and very challenging for children with HFASD. Therefore, we further suggest that the child with HFASD could be taught to look generally at a point of the "third eye" above and between the eyes in the middle of the forehead. This is a habit with which many people feel more comfortable. This is a centering and calming experience for both parties, often becoming unconscious with practice. It is important to recognize and convey to others that the child's lack of eye contact is not a sign of disrespect and, to some extent, may be difficult to modify.

The appropriate expression of affection depends upon the person's ability to differentiate between intimate friends and relatives and new acquaintances. These are social skills that require understanding of social rules of interpersonal relationships that can be taught and scripted to some extent.

Encouraging Achievement

Often, students' poor school performance may not be related to their disability alone—they also may be displaying underachievement. Frequently, we may be so careful to ensure protections for children with disabilities that we fail to set reasonable standards for them. We should look at the great achievements made by people like Helen Keller who have reached them against great odds. We are not suggesting that children should be pushed beyond their limits. Many persons unfamiliar with the complexities of special education issues may oversimplify problems with achievement by suggesting that "if she worked harder, she would be fine." Underachievement can be a problem at all ability levels, whether students have disabilities or not. It is important to remember that adults are responsible to some extent for their own happiness, but children require emotional protection and have a right to experience happiness. They also require moral, character, and spiritual guidance to make positive life choices. Commonly assumed markers of achievement should not violate children's rights for emotional protection, the experience of happiness, or the ability to think for themselves about their goals.

Home-Related Achievement Issues

Parental attitude in the home is key to encouraging school achievement. We hope we love our children unconditionally, but every child can be frustrating at times. For that reason, parents need to continually evaluate their feelings toward their child. At times, a parent may harbor feelings of rejection toward their child, which in turn are responsible for guilty feelings and irrational responses to the guilt. Are there barriers to maintaining and demonstrating unconditional love? Aim at conveying unconditional love to the child as much as possible, even when disagreeing, correcting behavior, or praising her. The child's behavior might be bad, but the child isn't. For too many children, shame results from feeling as though they are fundamentally bad. Shame, even for short periods, is one of the most destructive emotions a child can feel. Making a child with disabilities feel shame for something out of his control is abusive. There are parents whose ability to love their child is temporarily blocked due to their own concerns, anxieties, and frustrations. This is, in some way, to be expected when one is rearing a child with HFASD. Honesty with one's self is very important. There is no perfect way to feel about the situation. Just remember that love emerges when the truth is confronted honestly.

Every child can be seen as a unique gift with unique potential. Avoid comparing children. Let the child know that you see him as having a duty to know his own strengths and make his best efforts in and out of the classroom. Not every child can be the best at everything, but he can be his best at something. Many very competent children have low expectations for themselves because the bar has been set too low. This is especially the case in children with disabilities—too many parents are happy to see their children just getting by. If the child is currently an underachiever, convey the firm belief and expectation that she can learn and excel. By being a reasonable advocate, be sure that accommodations, supports, and special instructional strategies are in place to make learning easier, but do not relieve the child from her responsibility to make reasonable efforts. Know each child's strengths and weaknesses accurately as they emerge. Eventually, a child's strengths will emerge, coalesce, and integrate into a unique mix that many parents find they enjoy and treasure. Be sure that accommodations and school supports are enabling independence over dependence in learning.

Marital and family conflict can present roadblocks and resistance to emotional growth and motivation to learn. Parents should share their views and expectations of the child and family priorities. Never argue about the child in front of him. Seek to maximize points of agreement and learn to agree where you disagree. Put the "small stuff" aside. Make your discussions a safe place to forge a shared philosophy about child rearing. Try to be on the same page as much as possible about child rearing practices, rules, and consequences. When there are great disparities between parental expectations, children lock up or learn to fail as a way to passively punish parents for not communicating effectively. It is important for parents to get help for themselves when needed.

Other home-related ideas for encouraging achievement include:

» Try to eat one meal together daily as a family, and plan at-home family events such as regular game or movie nights.

» Success feels good. Children are born loving to learn and master challenges. Reward the child's successes with praise in a meaningful and genuine way so that she learns to know the feeling derived from mastering her challenges. Intrinsic incentives often are higher and more enduring rewards than prizes.

» Be patient with the child. A positive self-concept as a learner takes time for a child who has been experiencing little success. It may take a while before the positive experience of academic success takes hold.

» Limit television and video game time to one hour per weekday and 1 1/2 hours per weekend day. Telephone, instant messaging, and computer time should also have limits.

» Make sure the child gets adequate sleep by turning in nightly at a reasonable hour. Try not to break this rule on the weekends. There is great difficulty controlling television usage if one is located in the child's bedroom.

» Be open to mental health consultation for significant problems and to receiving parenting counseling. Attend support groups where available or help create one in your area.

» Make sure the child knows the rules for home behavior and responsibilities. Have the rules written out and posted in the child's room until she has mastered them.

» Develop a "To Do" list to post inside the child's bedroom door with a check-off system. Update this list weekly as the child receives assignments from school, or even daily.

» Remember that children see structure and limits as part of being loved. They are uncomfortable, confused, and even frightened without clear limits and expectations.
» Be a benevolent dictator first, and a friend later, when rules are established. Freedom should be earned through demonstrated responsibility.
» Model the behavior and values expected from the child in day-to-day activities, behavior, and conversation.
» Regularly demonstrate affection, especially with teenagers. Tell your child you love him regularly.
» Evaluate the openness of your communication with your child through regular conversations. Children need to feel your benign presence and acceptance through regular communication.

School-Related Achievement Issues

As a parent of a child with a disability, one should be in regular contact with the child's school. Try to keep one teacher, special educator, administrator, or counselor as a pivotal information conduit as a case manager. Use voicemail, e-mail, or any form of communication that is convenient for the school representative, and always communicate on an agreed-upon schedule for setting up meetings about your child. Establish good communication boundaries with your school representative and stick to them.

Parents should also set up homework rules and guidelines. Set regular study times every day for homework. Break up homework periods with dinner, snack, or exercise breaks. Also be sure to encourage the child to communicate about homework problems or questions with friends through telephone, instant messaging, or study groups.

A parent's attitude toward school can make all the difference in a child's achievement. Convey that school is an honorable place, that teachers are worthy of respect, and that school achievement is their major job, second only to being a good human being. If possible, volunteer to help out at school if you can. Volunteering at school will show your child that you value school as a part of your community.

Other ideas for improving school achievement at home include:

» Attend school functions, including Back to School Night and teacher/parent conference.

» Stay on top of child's needs by obtaining solid data about her progress. This might be supplied by tracking progress on work samples, regular school testing, or individualized psychological and/or educational assessments.

» Home responsibilities and chores are important, but should take second place to homework.

» At night, place everything needed for the next day's schoolwork next to the front door (or back) in the child's backpack, so it can't be forgotten the next morning.

» Check that the child has homework. If the child is lying about homework, that should be taken seriously. It may indicate that she is overwhelmed and having trouble asking for help.

» Read to or with the young child every night. And, let him see you reading at home.

» Directly explain the importance of good grades as a pathway to achievement in obtaining life's long-term rewards.

» Encourage the child to be unafraid to associate with and play with high-achieving children. You have a right to express your approval or concern about your child's friends.

» Encourage the child to have extracurricular activities at school. Concentrate on activities that the child actually enjoys to make school a desirable place to be.

Overall, remember that parents are their child's first and most important teachers. Parenting is a great art, as well as responsibility. Parents do play a key role in helping children adjust and master their worlds. This can be particularly challenging when the symptoms of HFASD inhibit practical, functional daily adjustment. Parents are to be commended for their efforts, flexibility, perseverance, and creativity in child rearing with kids who present challenges. They need to also realize that they cannot do it all alone and need to network, utilize, and create community supports for their children. Children, especially those with learning differences or challenges, do not come with a manual, but child-rearing can be the most rewarding of life experiences.

chapter 9

Transition to The World of Work, Independent Living, and College

What a relief and a joy it was to see Ben's acceptance into the University of Miami as a transfer student for his junior year of college! He would be majoring in engineering, his area of interest, passion, and talent. His 2 years at Brevard Community College in Florida had been extremely successful. Working closely with the school's disabilities coordinator, Ben had drafted a letter to each of his professors at the beginning of each semester telling them that he had HFASD and describing his unique strengths and needs. These teachers, who had been handpicked by the disabilities coordinator, were very receptive to allowing any and all of the accommodations that Ben might need, such as always giving instruction, directions, and assignments visually. Just knowing that he could stop in and see the disabilities coordinator for support had been a great relief to Ben, as well.

Despite all of Ben's success, his future still remained somewhat uncertain. He clearly still needed support with social skills and, although he had learned to take care of himself, he still preferred to live at home. He would continue to face great challenges as he went forward into his years at the University of Miami and beyond into his career and independent adult life.

HFASD is a lifelong condition. It does not end when high school is completed. We have previously pointed out the dangers of failing to diagnose HFASDs early and accurately, and many of the negative experiences suffered by adults whose needs have never been adequately addressed. With appropriate intervention and planning, individuals with HFASD can go on to be successful in postsecondary education, satisfying careers, and independent living. This requires well-planned transition. It is important to acknowledge that HFASD, while still by definition at the higher range, also represents its own range of severity. Some individuals will require few or no supports, while others may need more.

Transition Planning and Building Skills for Independent Living

Transition is one of the most poorly explored developmental services in schooling and the IEP process. The interface of self-knowledge, skill development, and world of work knowledge is poorly understood. Due to many factors, such as the economy and technological advancement, the workplace's demands are constantly growing and shifting. The U.S. has moved from an industrial economy with hands-on, routine jobs that might have been suitable to a significant number of persons with disabilities into an economy that is robotic and digitized, but also ironically, more social, where humans are more engaged in a service economy. It is a world that depends more and more on social connectivity and information exchange—areas where persons with autism are at a disadvantage. On the other hand, many people with HFASD have major contributions to make regarding technology and other areas of work. The trick is to prepare for the transition from high school so that the person with HFASD is able to share his gifts effectively.

What is transition? Transition to what? What are the purposes and goals of transition? Persons with HFASDs will be transitioning to such options as postsecondary education, independent living, employment, and service eligibility. The next big step for every parent and child is the identification of functionally realistic choices. This requires a great deal of preparation. Inevitably parents are asking or should be asking the following questions:

» Will my child be able to live independently?
» Will she go to college?
» How long will we, as parents, be absorbing financial responsibility for his life beyond secondary education?
» Will she be able to earn a living?
» What support services are available for individuals entering adulthood in our community?
» What legal eligibilities, entitlements, and rights does he have?

For the parent, these questions can be as stressful as the first diagnosis of their young child.

It is very important that parents ensure the quality of the transition plan in their child's IEP. Transition goals and objectives are required by law to have the same format and measurability as academic goals. Formal assessments must be conducted to determine an appropriate transition plan. Parents need to review the IEP to ensure that legal requirements are met. And once IEP transition goals have been written, appropriate services must be added to achieve them. More schools, public and private, are employing full or part-time "transition specialists," who work with parents, outside agencies, and businesses, and participate on IEP teams. Schools may utilize outside service providers if necessary, and in some jurisdictions, the school transition specialist can help arrange for a state Vocational Rehabilitation (VR) counselor to attend IEP meetings. As much as possible, the student herself should be consciously and actively involved in her own transition plan. She needs to be present at IEP meetings when transition is discussed and needs to take ownership of her own future as it progresses from fantasy, to written plan, to reality. Basic transition planning is required to start no later than age 16 on IEP teams, but some may begin services as early as age 14.

Fortunately, in the United States, most parents and service providers are aware of the child's right to FAPE. But when a student leaves public education in the U.S., she leaves a world of entitlements and enters a world of eligibilities. With eligibilities, there are few guarantees. Under the Individuals with Disabilities Education Act (IDEA), students with disabilities are entitled to services until they either graduate with a regular diploma or age out of the system at age 21. After the young adult with HFASD leaves the public school system, the right to services doesn't exist. For this reason, families should consider carefully whether a diploma at 18 years of age or a nondiploma track that allows the student to remain in school until 21 years of age is the best choice for their child. Eligibilities vary from program to program and from state to state. Simply having an ASD categorization on an IEP does not guarantee adult services. Transition planning is critical in dealing with these issues.

Readiness for transition options is based on many diagnostic and developmental factors. Proper vocational planning involves knowledge of these developmental considerations:

» level of general intellectual ability;
» specific intellectual skills such as verbal ability, numerical reasoning, visual/spatial reasoning, memory, and speed of processing;

» level of adaptive skills for self-care and independent living;
» academic skill area strengths and weaknesses;
» temperament and personality factors;
» executive function skills;
» attention skills;
» emotional maturity;
» basic behavioral controls for the workplace;
» knowledge of self;
» vocational interests;
» knowledge of the world of work;
» knowledge of specific educational requirements for certification for a job;
» knowledge of programs for certification in a given job skill;
» social skills for job performance (i.e., the ability to take supervision and work with peers);
» workplace hygiene; and
» the ability to advocate for one's self.

Parents need to understand that transition involves the emergence and development of a great many of the skills cited above. In autism, there may be a great deal of variability in the emergence of skill sets and some skills may be "stuck" by the disability. There is also a sense of general intellectual, social, and emotional immaturity in many children with disabilities. They may think and respond emotionally as a younger person might. Tasks should be planned based on skill level and not chronological age. Too often, when children with disabilities are asked about their future job interests, it is based on a simple interest inventory or simple fantasy: "I want to be a doctor" or "I want to be a video game programmer." Career choices should be grounded in knowledge of personal strengths and weaknesses, the educational requirements, the economic climate, or the industries in which these professions are found.

One important way of assessing a person's readiness for various postsecondary challenges is the measurement of "adaptive behavior" or the incremental attainment of skills for self-care and independent living in critical domains. There are psychological tests that are used to evaluate the development of persons on hierarchical scales of independent functioning. Generally, they assess the following domains:

» communication (e.g., giving clear directions, sustaining a conversation, stating needs appropriately);
» daily living skills (e.g., independent hygiene skills, shopping, cooking, transportation, money management);
» socialization (e.g., attending a weekly group activity, avoiding embarrassing or antagonizing others); and
» motor skills.

When summarizing the student's readiness upon exiting secondary school education, it is wise to make a prioritized list or draw a chart or other visual picture to demonstrate the student's developmental strengths and weaknesses for independent living and employment based on the above areas of development. Getting an up-to-date assessment of the child's adaptive skills at 14 or 15 years of age can be very helpful as you set the priorities for a transition plan throughout high school.

Independent Living

Better adaptive skills should lead to success in independent living. Life for adults with HFASD without early diagnosis and preparation can be a struggle. Engström, Ekström, and Emilsson (2003), in a Swedish study of adult adjustment, reported that the majority of their subjects were living independently, and all but one was unemployed. None were married and none had children. Only a few had a partner. Most persons needed a high level of public and/or private support. The overall adjustment was rated good in 12%, fair in 75%, and poor in 12% of the population studied. The authors concluded that persons with HFASD have extensive need for support from their families and society. We have mentioned earlier that there are risks for adults who have not had proper diagnosis and supports throughout their lives. Because HFASD is only recently being recognized and standardized as a diagnostic category, there are many adults in their 40s and older who have not benefited from clarity in diagnostic identification or the recent explosion of interest and knowledge in this area.

In other studies, among high-functioning adults with HFASD, 22% (Howlin, Goode, Hutton, & Rutter, 2004) and 27% (Cederlund, Hagberg, Billstedt, Gillberg, & Gillberg, 2008) were rated as attaining "very good" or "good" outcomes in terms of independence, friendships/steady relationship, and education and/or job. Marriage, Wolverton, and Marriage (2009) reported a very wide range of outcomes in their sample of 80 high-functioning adults, from an isolated individual living on disability pension to a married university professor. Most were functioning well below their potential, as indicated by their IQs. There were many social and sensory challenges reported in the workplace. There were significant challenges in executive functioning. In a survey of 68 adults (ages 21–48) in the UK with autism and IQs above 50 (Howlin et al., 2004), 58% were rated as having poor or very poor outcomes; 8 were competitively employed; 1 was self-employed but earned below a living wage; 14 worked in supported, sheltered, or volunteer jobs; and 42 were in programs or had chores through a residential provider.

Outcome studies indicate that the large majority of adults with HFASD are either unemployed or underemployed. Individuals with HFASD are far more likely to lose their jobs or not progress because of social reasons than an inability to do the job task.

Employment

It takes great art to be a "matchmaker" for today's workers with HFASD in a changing world of work. This kind of matchmaking cannot be achieved with a one-time administration of a simple interest inventory given by a high school counselor or transition specialist. Decisions must be made upon weighing many factors, which include the level of supervision during training and on the job. What is the best work environment for a person with a HFASD? Because people with HFASD bring unique strengths and challenges to the work force, identifying the best fit between the person and the job is important and requires careful consideration. Many of the manifestations found in the diagnostic classification of HFASD can be translated into work behaviors or preferences. Table 1 provides a list of these behaviors.

Another source of information that can help guide employment decisions is an up-to-date psychological evaluation. American public school students with disabilities who have an IEP are entitled to a review or reevaluation by a psychologist every 3 years. A school psychologist usually conducts these. Sometimes requisite annual or triennial reviews result in no new actual testing of the student. Students can change dramatically in developmental periods between one testing review and another. It is imperative that a student exits school with proper documentation to enter the world of work and independent living. Many school districts do not encourage triennial retesting in 10th through 12th grades or before a student earning a certificate (and not a diploma) reaches age 21. This documentation can be critical for the eligibility requirements of postsecondary training opportunities. Not every student needs to be tested every year or every 3 years as special education law permits. But, when appropriate, a student nearing the end of public education should be tested if that information reflects her current stage of

TABLE 1.
Work-Related Behaviors

Here are some work-related problems taken from the social characteristics list by Roger Meyer and Tony Attwood (2001) often faced by persons with AS:

- Difficulty with teamwork.
- Deliberate withholding of peak performance due to belief that one's best efforts may remain unrecognized, unrewarded, or appropriated by others.
- Intense pride in expertise or performance, often perceived by others as "flouting behavior."
- Sarcasm, negativism, criticism.
- Difficulty in accepting compliments, often responding with quizzical or self-deprecatory language.
- Tendency to lose it during sensory overload, multitask demands, or when contradictory and confusing priorities have been set.
- Difficulty in starting projects.
- Discomfort with competition, out of scale reactions to losing.
- Low motivation to perform tasks of no immediate personal interest.
- Oversight or forgetting of tasks without formal reminders such as lists or schedules.
- Great concern about order and appearance of personal work area.
- Slow performance.
- Perfectionism.
- Difficulty with unstructured time.
- Reluctance to ask for help or seek comfort.
- Excessive questions.
- Low sensitivity to risks in the environment to self and/or others.
- Difficulty with writing and reports.
- Reliance on internal speech process to talk oneself through a task or procedure.
- Stress, frustration, and angry reaction to interruptions.
- Difficulty in negotiating, either in conflict situations or as a self-advocate.
- Very low level of assertiveness.
- Reluctance to accept positions of authority or supervision.
- Strong desire to coach or mentor newcomers.

> **TABLE 1.** *Continued*
> - Difficulty in handling relationships with authority figures.
> - Often viewed as vulnerable or less able to resist harassment and badgering by others.
> - Punctual and conscientious.
> - Avoids socializing, "hanging out," or small talk on and off the job. (Meyer & Attwood, 2001, p. 306)
>
> *Note.* From *School Success for Kids With Asperger's Syndrome* (pp. 171–172) by S. M. Silverman and R. Weinfeld, 2007, Waco, TX: Prufrock Press. Copyright 2007 by Prufrock Press. Reprinted with permission.

development and her readiness for the challenges in the next stage in her life effectively.

Once an accurate assessment has been conducted of the student, usually by a certified school psychologist, licensed psychologist, or neuropsychologist, combined with related service assessments (speech-language, occupational therapy) as needed, then basic work readiness factors can be determined. These may include preemployment and work maturity measures like the Pre-Employment/Work Maturity Checklists and Workforce Performance Rating checklists developed by Strumpf Associates: Center for Strategic Change. These evaluate basic work attitudes and skills and actual performance on the job.

Some general tips for finding jobs for and helping people with HFASD succeed in the workplace include:

» Be systematic with the job search with a sequential step-by-step plan.
» Provide support in the development of a good resume.
» Prepare good references.
» Help the individual think creatively to transform his special interests and talents into marketable skills.
» Concretely practice job-related social skills (e.g., interviews, what to do at lunch, how to interact differently with boss vs. peers vs. supervisees, asking for help, grooming and presentation, etc.).

» Help the applicant communicate his challenges to administration and coworkers in a congenial and matter-of-fact manner (given deficits in theory of mind).

» Provide coaching to review challenges, successes, and failures in the workplace through regular, systematic analysis and practice.

» Don't fade the job coaching too quickly. Make sure that the person with HFASD is consistently and independently managing all of the demands of the job and feels comfortable before beginning a slow process of fading supports.

Just like many of us, people with HFASD can face both advantages and struggles in the workplace. You may need to help advocate for their ability to be a good employee, reminding the employer of some of the potential advantages of an HFASD employee, including:

» timeliness;
» may do work that others find too repetitive;
» not likely to waste time in office gossip or politics;
» technological skills;
» attention to detail;
» logical, analytical problem solving; and
» strong commitment to job.

Some common potential challenges in the workplace for persons with HFASD are:

» social problems,
» sensory issues,
» slow processing, and
» trouble handling changes in rules/job requirements/perceived unfairness.

Job Coaching

A job coach can:

» gradually prepare the person for the nuances and social demands of the workplace. Some behaviors will serve to annoy coworkers and may result in termination. It is best to teach behaviors appropriate to specific places of employment while in the natural setting;

» help the person develop standard operating procedures and routines for completing work, handling special requests, communicating with colleagues, etc.;

» teach the person appropriate hygiene and dress for specific work settings;

» instruct about social interchanges around appropriate topics that can assist with office small talk and during job-related discussions. Initial preparation of the job site can avoid unnecessary difficulties and promote long-term success;

» identify a mentor to whom the person can turn for assistance and advice; and

» consider safe and efficient means of transportation and help to establish routes, schedules, and other important information.

Job coaches can help, but ultimately, chances of success are optimized in many cases if someone at work can provide needed prompts on site. Goals of intervention are often to both teach social skills and make sure there is a social support network in the places where the individual spends the most time (e.g., home, work, neighborhood, recreation places, etc.). This works best when there is a community of supportive individuals. This has sometimes been effective in group living situations when people with the same challenges support each other with trained guidance in the living quarters.

Legal Protections in the Workplace

Many important laws have influenced transition to adult services. The Americans with Disabilities Act (ADA) was enacted to ensure that people with disabilities have accommodations to access public places and activities. There was also the 1999 Supreme Court ruling in *Olmstead v. L. C.*, which requires states to "provide services to persons with disabilities in community settings rather than institutions, if certain conditions are met" in order to comply with the ADA. This primarily addresses those with severe disabilities, who need long-term institutional or nursing home care, and who have Medicaid.

Although the Americans with Disabilities Act protects adults with HFASD where accommodations are required, they may not be entitled to services they may need to succeed in those environments. For example, if an adult with HFASD needs assistance to get and keep a job, he or she must first qualify and then apply for specific vocational services provided by the state Vocational Rehabilitation agency. There are 80 such agencies throughout the U.S., operating under the Federal Rehabilitation Services Administration. Each agency is funded by approximately 80% federal and 20% state monies. Each agency office may provide a range of services to include: job training, assistive technology, job placement, interest assessments, and job coaching, for example. The applicant, however, must show that he or she:

» has a physical or mental impairment that substantially interferes in his or her ability to work (with proper medical documents);

» needs vocational services to obtain and retain employment; and

» is intending that any VR service requested or received must be directly related to obtaining and keeping employment.

The application for services is reviewed by a VR counselor who determines eligibility and informs the applicant of the decision. Whenever the VR agency lacks funds for all eligible applicants, the agency may implement an "Order of Selection" (actually a waiting list), which is based on three tiers of need. The first tier includes eligible people with two or more significant disabilities. The second includes eligible people with one significant disability, while the third is for people with less significant disabilities. Under such circumstances, an eligible person with strong intellectual abilities, such as individuals with HFASD, may not get vocational services. This is an example where eligibility for services does not result in obtaining services.

Similarly, many persons with HFASD with college degrees have been informed that they are too intellectually superior to qualify for developmental disabilities services. Yet, due to the core symptoms of ASD, they are often too socially impaired to obtain and keep a job on their own. They are then faced with federally defined poverty levels and must apply for social services and Medicaid or apply for unemployment. This is clearly a case of "falling through the cracks" in the system.

As a result of these gaps in services and current economic conditions, nonprofit agencies, universities, philanthropic foundations, and civic-minded companies often provide jobs. This can be accomplished by convincing large corporations that persons with HFASD have skills and a passion to succeed in areas of employment that others may not find as engaging.

How to Request Workplace Resources

We know what an educational accommodation is from Chapters 5, 6, and 7. But what is a workplace accommodation? It is any modification to the work environment or a process in which work is conducted. An accommodation can apply to any aspect of employment, from hiring to orientation training, to participation in workplace activities. Accommodations can also include modification in work schedules, policies, physical changes in the workspace, operational equipment, job task restructuring, supervisory techniques, and job coaching. The aim is to help an individual with a disability apply for a job, perform the job's duties, and to enjoy the process and privileges of working. The Americans with Disabilities Act (ADA) states that employers are required to make reasonable accommodations for an employee with a disability, as long as the accommodation does not pose an "undue hardship" to the employer. Factors considered under hardship include the:

» nature and cost of the accommodation;
» resources and size of the business;
» type of business—composition, functions, workforce structure; and
» impact the accommodation would have on the facility and business as a whole.

Reasonable accommodation does not require lowering performance standards or removing essential functions of the individual's job. Persons with disabilities who are prospective employees should find out if there are already accommodations in place. Persons with HFASD will need to request accommodations if they are not already being utilized. This requires that they must disclose the disabling condition. They should ask the following questions about disclosing their disability:

» What are the benefits, risks, and new workplace perceptions?
» Should the disability and its impact be disclosed immediately, or after some time on the job?
» Who needs to know about the disability and what will be the effect on coworkers?
» What is the easiest way to introduce the disability and need for accommodations to leadership and coworkers?

According to the law, one only needs to inform the employer that an adjustment is needed due to a medical condition. Simple, concrete language is best. The individual can first ask for feedback about how his performance is progressing. He might request breaks or written visual schedules and reminders of routines. This should all be done collaboratively as referred to by the ADA as an "interactive process." He needs to be clear about the request. Many workplace accommodations are available such as tablet or smartphone apps. The Equal Employment Opportunities Commission (EEOC) is a federal agency responsible for enforcing the employment provisions of the ADA. If an accommodation request is denied, a worker can appeal the decision by filing a grievance with their union or with a state's enforcing agency of the EEOC itself.

A workplace most suitable and ideal for persons with HFASD:

» is quiet and predictable and allows for sensory retreats;
» is low in social demands;
» provides a great deal of explicit supervision from a knowledgeable, caring boss;
» is where a special, more technical, or concrete skill or interest is employed;
» is where there is less need for "common sense" or engaging in conventional judgment; and
» is where time or productivity pressures are relatively low.

When Competitive Employment Is Not an Option

For some adults with HFASD, competitive full-time employment may not be a realistic option, because the right match is not available, no workplace is able or willing to provide the accommodations, or the kind of supervision required for success is lacking. Others may require additional preparation or special preemployment experiences before they are ready for part- or full-time employment in a workplace. Some adults can work effectively from home with supervision.

Some fail repeatedly despite having advanced degrees or superior skills or knowledge. A weak work ethic or poor work habits are not the source of the problem. Adults with HFASD are in the job market, trying hard but still not getting the job, or getting fired repeatedly for lack of social skills or other job maintenance skills.

Some individuals with HFASD may suffer from coexisting conditions that affect their performance or the way they are perceived, such as anxiety, depression, OCD, ADHD, tics, or seizures. By themselves these symptoms or conditions might not be disabling, but they may make their work more challenging when in combination with HFASD.

Some are overwhelmed or even injured by the stress of coping with an uncongenial work environment, and/or by their repeated work failures. When someone has had several work failures and has experienced a significant decrease in their physical or psychological health because of work-related stress, they may require relief from work expectations in order to have some balance or quality of life. For them, it may be necessary to consider alternative financial or supervisory supports.

It may also be clear that certain young adults with minimal or no previous work attempts may not initially succeed at employment. This is why prevocational assessment and preparation is so important—to avoid the experience of undue failure.

As early-diagnosed and early-treated children with HFASD come of age, we hope that tomorrow's adults with HFASD will be better prepared to enter the workplace. Presently, many adults are connecting with the HFASD diagnosis, which was not available to them as children, because they are seeking explanations for and assistance with their problems in the workplace from clinicians in the mental health arena. Because of early diagnosis and intervention, increasing numbers of those with HFASD are being appropriately prepared for and can experience success in the workspace.

Temple Grandin and Kate Duffy (2008) have written on the topic of careers particularly suited for persons with HFASD. Another popular spokesperson for people on the autism spectrum is John Elder Robison (2011), who has written about independent living, learning, and working as a person with an HFASD. Some of the fields in which people with HFASD typically excel are engineering, science, mathematics, and computer related fields, as well as many others.

Travel Training and Driving

Independent mobility is an important goal for individuals with HFASD. Consideration for which mobility method to use should be based on factors such as maturity, mentor/family support, and the ability to execute daily living skills. Walking, cycling, using transit, and driving are all viable options, however, only to be selected after a careful assessment and accompanied by individualized travel or operator training. A Potential to Drive (PTD) assessment should be administered by a specialized program or professional such as an occupational therapist and/or Certified Driver Rehabilitation Specialist who understand the HFASD driving profile. The following eight factors (Monahan & Classen, 2013) should be assessed during the PTD process and trained as necessary:

- » motor coordination;
- » prioritization of information;
- » attentional shifting;
- » developing and implementing a plan;
- » generalizing skills to different environments (socialization);
- » anticipating actions and intentions of other drivers;
- » self-monitoring;
- » hazard recognition;
- » reaction time;
- » judgment, especially after an accident; and
- » frustration tolerance.

When considering training your child on driving skills, you might want to check into the following resources:

» Driver Rehabilitation Institute is a nonprofit organization that provides education, mentoring, and tools for occupational therapy professionals working in the field of driver rehabilitation and has good tips and resources for driving training: http://www.driverrehabinstitute.org

» The "Driving and Aspergers: Balancing Independence and Safety" video is a helpful introduction to what to do with your young driver: http://vimeo.com/35717803

Finding a Social Network

Social opportunities and networks are important, not just for therapeutic improvement in social skills, but to enjoy recreation, sports, and quality of life in a social environment. Otherwise, too much time can be spent withdrawn in solitary activities. In a recent study, Mazurek and Engelhardt (2013) found that boys with ASD played video games for significantly longer periods each day than typically developing boys—an average of 2.1 hours versus 1.2 hours. Furthermore, boys with ASD who often played role-playing video games were more likely to be oppositional compared to boys with ASD who played other types of games. Also, boys with ASD who preferred role-playing and/or first-person shooter video games were more likely to display problematic patterns of video game use. This was a correlational study and not one that explored cause and effect. Do more oppositional children choose video gaming to the exclusion of other activities or do role-playing games lead to oppositional behavior?

In 2013, the advocacy group Autism Speaks conducted a national survey on community youth organizations. The survey assessed the needs and wants of parents/caregivers of youth with autism in the area of youth organizations. Of the 1,018 respondents, 83% were parents of males and 17% were parents of females with autism. The study resulted in the publication of *Leading the Way: Autism-Friendly Youth Organization Guide*. When asked about the organized youth activities they would like made available to their youth, team sports and camping/ outdoor adventure topped the list.

The key unmet needs families experience in relation to youth organizations were:

» staff educated on autism and trained on effective interventions to help people with autism,
» programs and/or summer camps offering adaptive services for people with autism,
» affordable programs, and
» opportunities for socialization with neurotypical youth.

The top barriers that families experience to having their child participate in a youth organization were (Autism Speaks, 2013):

» no programs specifically designed for youth with autism (55%);
» lack of behavior management services (50%);
» untrained staff (50%); and
» expense of the program, lack of scholarships (48%).

Survey respondents felt the key training needs for youth organizations to address were behavior management, tips for working with people with autism, communication strategies, and activity safety risks like wandering, hypothermia, drowning, etc. (Autism Speaks, 2013).

Specific therapeutic interventions for social skills are provided in Chapter 4. Academic interventions are provided in Chapter 6. Social networks exist through cyberspace. Formerly and currently referring to themselves as "Aspies," people have communicated with each other through a number of online forums. Group living for persons with HFASD may have social skills training experiences or indirect benefits through the implied mutual support of having a shared diagnosis.

Succeeding in College

College administrators have begun to educate themselves about accommodating for the increase of students with HFASD entering their programs. Best practices are just being developed. Soon, increasing successes will be seen through graduation and other outcome measures that will demonstrate if new college programs and accommodations are working. College websites are increasingly displaying accommodation options for persons with HFASD in their disability support departments.

Community colleges are particularly affected by an influx of students with HFASD. Many students are hesitant about their ability to handle 4 years of college. However, many students who would have been fearful of attending any college in the past are attending 2-year colleges. Community college classes are often smaller than at universities, and tuition costs are much lower. In addition to regular academic courses, most offer "personal development" classes that can be very helpful for students with HFASD, such as introduction to college, study skills, friendship, self-esteem, career exploration, etc. Many students attend a community college as a stepping stone to a 4-year college, some may want to earn a 2-year associate's degree, and some may want to just sample a variety of courses of personal or vocational interest.

Having IEPs and 504 plans and being prepared to advocate for themselves, many students with HFASD are now taking on the challenge of higher education. Students with HFASD need different supports than those that have been available to students with learning disabilities in the past, which colleges find most familiar. Just as in any part of the learning process, highly individualized programs and supports are required for each student. But in the absence of IEPs and entitlements, individualization is more limited and students are forced to adjust with what is available in a community that is expected to be more independent. This absence of wraparound support does not work for every student. Even for students without disabilities, many

4-year colleges have a significant dropout and transfer rate after the freshman year.

When applying for supports, college students can be required to supply documentation demonstrating their current disability and need for academic adjustment or auxiliary aid or service. A copy of an IEP can be critical, as well as psychological and other evaluations, which have been conducted at least within a 3-year period. It is not uncommon for psychologists working in this field to receive referrals from adults who have never been tested and have no prior special education experience. Obtaining accommodations for college boards (SAT/ACT), medical school entrance exam (MCAT), law school exams (LSAT), and other entrance tests can be challenging. These applications may be rebuffed. Negotiation may be required with board authorities. It is always best to have a history of regular evaluations and copies of school IEPs. Many students enter college without even contacting the disability office. The following are some typical and some sophisticated accommodations for participation in college:

- » extended time on tests for students with slow comprehension or processing rates;
- » copies of lecturer daily lessons;
- » copies of other students' notes;
- » a note taker;
- » use of word processor for all assignments and tests;
- » text-to-speech processing and other assistive technology aids as needed;
- » reduced course load;
- » early registration for classes to help create a schedule that works with the student's needs (i.e., no early morning classes if that interferes with a specific time to take medications or scheduling around effects of medication);
- » a self-advocacy note to each professor;
- » preferential seating;
- » writing on test forms;
- » tests with less distracting stimulation;
- » a separate testing center when required;

» syllabi that make all of the expectations of the course completely explicit;
» training in the hidden curriculum for how to participate in a seminar; and
» provision of virtual and real meeting spaces for people with HFASDs.

A good resource for students with HFASD planning to attend college is the book *Realizing the College Dream With Autism or Asperger's Syndrome* (Palmer, 2006), which provides advice on how to get into college and how to adjust to the college lifestyle and educational demands. There are basic life skills that are required to negotiate college. These are not necessarily covered as accommodations by colleges and are "expected" in a college student. They include:

» executive functioning, especially organizational skills, including the ability to manage unstructured time and create calendars and to do lists;
» self-advocacy;
» independent living skills;
» ability to share a dorm room or the wisdom to request a single room if required;
» self-medication skills—knowing the name of all medications, who prescribed them, what they do, what to do when the student is running out of medications;
» map reading—navigating a college campus, allowing sufficient time to get to class;
» social skills for college life (i.e., attending campus events, forming peer study groups, joining clubs or activities, dating);
» problem-solving strategies;
» utilization of campus resources;
» maintaining concentration and avoiding the distractions of college; and
» forming a study group of appropriate peers.

There are also basic behavioral protocol skills for college classroom participation such as:

» clearly understanding classroom expectations,
» knowing when to ask a question,
» knowing what you can do if you still don't understand,
» understanding appropriate classroom participation, and
» understanding unstated classroom procedures (hidden curriculum).

Some students do not have these skills and require private supports. The following are examples of some support programs for higher education for persons with HFASDs, which can be viewed on their websites:

» The TEACCH centers of North Carolina: http://www.teacch.com

» The College Internship Program: http://www.cipworldwide.org

» The College Living Experience (CLE): http://experiencecle.com

» AHEADD: http://www.aheadd.org

» Spectrum College Transition Program: http://www.spectrumcollegetransition.org

The following are general tips for students with HFASD attending regular colleges and universities:

» Inform your advisor that you have special needs.
» Go to the office responsible for disability programs or services, introduce yourself, and find out what you must do to be eligible for services and what is available. It will be much easier to receive help later if you need it.
» Exercise care in selecting classes at registration with the help of your advisor. Ask for help in choosing small, structured classes with professors who use multisensory methods of instruction, provide a syllabus, and present

information clearly and in an organized fashion. Be encouraged to choose instructors who provide visual as well as auditory input during lectures and through the use of chalkboards, overheads, and written handouts.

» Inform your professors of your needs early in the semester (or ask for help from your advisor or disability office). Most professors will be receptive to your needs if alerted to them before there is a problem.

» Ask questions of professors during their regular office hours.

» Participate in class discussions. This can bring up your grade if you have trouble with tests.

» Attend all quiz and review sessions. If possible, join or create a study group to discuss and review material for each course.

» Make use of tutorial services immediately if you have trouble with the content of a course or if you need help in structuring an assignment.

» Recording lectures is sometimes beneficial if you have time to listen to them later. Be aware, however, that some devices do not pick up every little sound and thus can be difficult to understand at times. If you do decide to use a recording device, make certain that it has a counter. You can then record the exact number of an important point when you are seeking clarification of your own notes and will not need to listen to the entire tape. It is always important to continue to take notes, both to help maintain your attention and to facilitate development of this skill.

» The Livescribe pen is an example of an effective method for recording notes and drawings on special paper. Later the student can touch the note and hear what the teacher was saying.

» Index cards are excellent aids for memorization of facts (one per card—use them like flash cards until you know them. Return to them later for review before tests). They are also useful in organizing notes for a paper.

» Establish a set time and place to study. Because this should be relatively free from distractions, it may mean going to the library.

» Use a large calendar to plot due dates and daily increments of assignments. Be sure to place all other important activities on the calendar also so that you may plan around them.

» Use counseling services to coach you and to review the sources of insecurities for the purpose of strengthening confidence and building resilience to potential emotional life-stressors at college.

Some colleges, like Arizona State University (ASU), have started a one-credit class for students with HFASD: Autism Spectrum Disorders Higher Ed. This course is specifically designed to benefit students with HFASD. The course focuses on reading "Aquamarine Blue," a collection of stories about the experiences and challenges of students with Asperger's syndrome living in college. This is a way for the students to discuss college challenges, talk about personal issues in a supportive environment, and try to develop friendships with other students. The students also formed an "Aspies at ASU" club.

There are a number of very helpful resources for college students with HFASD. One is a DVD available from the Organization for Autism Research entitled *Understanding Asperger's Syndrome: A Professor's Guide*. This DVD focuses on educating professors, teaching assistants, and others on what it means to be a college student on the spectrum and how they might best be able to help them succeed. It is only 12 minutes in length but gives an introduction to life as a college student with Asperger's syndrome. It allows students to practice self-advocacy by identifying needed and reasonable accommodations to help them be successful. Students can provide the video to their professors either in a DVD or by providing a link to the video via the Internet.

In addition to college financial aid packages, students can seek funding for tuition from the federal Vocational Rehabilitation program if their courses will help them to become "competitively employed."

Creating a Secure Adulthood

Looking toward adulthood, parents should prepare themselves through the transition process by becoming informed about:

» Social Security and other government benefits including Social Security Disability Insurance, and

» estate planning, including trusts and other arrangements as parents age and are less able to support their dependent or partially dependent young adult with disabilities.

Looking forward to secure financial adulthood provides great comfort that the child's quality of life will be protected when parents are no longer able to provide supervision or active monitoring of resources and support. We've included a long list of resources to help your child with independent living and the world of work, along with guidance for examining Social Security options and estate planning in Appendix F.

chapter 10

Conclusion

School Success for Kids With HFASD

Sue Klingshirn, autism consultant for the Medina City School District in Ohio, first met Ethan when he was in fourth grade. His classroom teachers were reporting his inability to begin work and stay on task, his lack of organization, and his problems with social skills. It was around this time that Ethan was identified by a school psychologist and the school's IEP team as a student with HFASD who needed an IEP. Sue included Ethan in a social skills group with other students at the elementary school. Ethan had a focused interest (some would call it an obsession) with cleaning. An individual contract was set up with Ethan where he could earn the "privilege" of cleaning Sue's room at the end of the day if he completed his class work with a certain number of prompts. Needless to say, Sue was very happy when Ethan met his goal!

Throughout middle school, Ethan progressed with the guidance and support of several wonderful special education teachers who received extra training and consultation from Sue and others on working with students who have HFASD. During this critical period of social development, Sue worked on social skills with Ethan three times a week. He was included in a group with two other students with HFASD. Neurotypical peers were brought in on a regular basis to help the students with HFASD with specific middle school social issues. For example, when a school dance was approaching, three girls worked with Ethan and his peer group on where to go, what to do, what to wear, and all the other "rules" of this social event. They even brought in examples of the music that would be played so that Ethan and the others would have a chance to get used to it. At other times during the year, the group practiced making phone calls to peers and talking to others about school and homework. Ethan learned the rules of meeting new people and entering into existing conversations. Beginning in eighth grade, Ethan began visiting the high school once a month to prepare for that huge transition.

Now in ninth grade, Ethan has done very well in his new school. He uses a laptop computer for his classwork and is now able to take his own notes. The older he gets, the fewer modifications he needs and receives. He has a new tablet with many useful applications. He is able to finish tests now with one extra class period. (In middle school, he once took 3 days to complete a test!) Ethan's teachers are trained in working with students with HFASD and receive support from Sue and other special educators in the school. Ethan responds very well to the wait time, visual accommodations, and organization structures that teachers use throughout his day. Ethan has clearly benefited from his daily social skills class, where he's learning the skills of how to work cooperatively in a team or group situation, how to deal with bullying, and how to navigate the world of dating. Ethan continues to work on improving his self-advocacy skills. One successful strategy has been for him to mark an "H" on any paper with which he is having difficulty, so that he can remember to ask for help later in the day from one of his special educators.

Ethan also reports that he has had a hard time making friends. He says that in the past he may have talked too much or not asked the other person enough questions. Although he is happy to have one trusted friend, he says it's difficult to make others because they may not be interested in his interests, which include cleaning, yard work, tractors, and trucks.

However, Ethan has come a long way since Sue met him in fourth grade. She feels that this has been a result of teamwork between his home and school environments. Sue talks about the fact that Ethan's parents have high expectations for him and advocate for what he needs, while always keeping in mind the big picture of moving him from dependence to independence over time.

It's easy to imagine from Ethan's example that Sue Klingshirn works tirelessly to make sure that all students with HFASD can successfully participate in their neighborhood high school, a school that serves 2,400 students. Sue has put a system in place that educates and supports staff so that students with HFASD can have their needs met in their classrooms throughout the day. She identifies general education staff members at each grade level who take the lead in providing appropriate education for these students. These designated teachers participate in training in order to learn about students with HFASD. Sue meets formally with all of these teachers every 2 weeks and is available for quick consultations on a daily basis. Dealing with sensory issues, as well as behavioral issues, are frequent topics of discussion in these meetings. In addition to Sue, an occupational therapist and a school psychologist typically attend these meetings and help solve problems and provide training. In addition to providing training to classroom teachers, all school staff in Medina City, including secretaries and bus drivers, also receive periodic training on the characteristics of students with HFASD, as well as the best practices for working with this special group of kids.

Classroom teachers learn that it is crucial to use visual supports for these students. They provide visual supports in their classes by always being sure to post the agenda for the day on the board, providing clear written instructions and directions, using colors to differentiate and designate important materials and concepts, and incorporating routines as simple as holding up the book or material to which they are orally referring. Sue says that if you ask the teachers about the most important accommodation that they use, most will speak about "wait time," or allowing each student time to process the question and information before responding. Interestingly, teachers report that the accommodations that are good for kids with HFASD also help many of the other kids, as well.

Students with HFASD in the Medina City program follow a typical schedule for a majority of their day. When needed, special education teachers may be in the general education classroom to coteach or to be available to support the students with HFASD. One important addition to the students' schedule is a special health class taught by an exceptional physical education teacher. In a small classroom environment, students work on social skills and school survival skills, as well as participate in adapted physical education activities with a limited number of neurotypical peers.

The success of Sue's program is not only due to the supports that students with HFASD receive once they enter high school, it is a culmination of work that has been done with the students since they were in elementary school. There is a careful transition put into place to prepare students to move from elementary to middle school and then from middle school to high school. After participating in prep time in their middle school, eighth-grade students with HFASD come to the high school once a month. They learn to navigate the halls, eat lunch in the crowded and noisy cafeteria, learn the locations of the classes that they will take upon arriving in high school, and even gain experience with these classes by sitting in on them.

The Medina City program for kids with HFASD is one outstanding example. Whether students are supported in the general education program, as described in the example of the Medina City program; whether they are attending special classes within a general education school, as described in the example of the Montgomery County program in Chapter 6; or whether they are attending special schools, as described in the example of the Ivymount School in Chapter 7, it is crucial that school staff members are trained in the best practices for educating this population.

When educators and parents work as a team, employing the best practices described in this book and doing so in the best interests of students with HFASD, it is clear that these students can and will experience school success. HFASD has no cure, but with the use of proper supports and strategies in the home and school environment to help them overcome their weaknesses and build their confidence as successful students, individuals with HFASD can live happy, successful lives.

The intensity of supports afforded each individual will vary. Although students with HFASD face significant challenges, with early and effective intervention they can be expected to live lives that are personally satisfying and that make contributions to our society as a whole.

Since the publication of *School Success for Kids With Asperger's Syndrome* in 2006, there has been increased interest, research, and discussion. Now, since the publication of the DSM-5 in May 2013, the term "Asperger's syndrome" has been eliminated and subsumed under the new definition of "autistic spectrum disorder" or ASD. For the purpose of this book, we have been referring to people who are higher functioning as HFASD. We have learned more about the genetics of autism, the neurological systems associated with the various behavioral differences found in ASD. We have learned more about coexisting conditions (comorbidities) such as attention, anxiety, and other challenges.

We have especially learned about executive functioning problems and "theory of mind" in perspective taking.

More and more postsecondary options are opening up for persons with HFASD, and more supports are being utilized to help with life transitions to the world of work and independent living. Parents have been given more tools for financial planning. More persons with HFASDs are being identified earlier, and being met with appropriate interventions earlier. We are learning more about how to support better futures for persons with HFASD as they enter adulthood.

We hope that this book has been helpful in demystifying HFASD and in providing tools for early identification and intervention in schools and the community so that your student with HFASD can also find success.

References

Alvord, M., Zucker, B., & Grados, J. (2011).
*Resilience builder program for children and
adolescents: Enhancing social competence and
self-regulation.* Champaign, IL: Research
Press.

Americans with Disabilities Act, 42 U.S.C. §§
12102 et seq. (1990).

Americans with Disabilities Act Amendments
Act of 2008 € 3(4)(E)(i). 42 U.S.C. €
12102(4)(E).

American Psychiatric Association. (2000).
*Diagnostic and statistical manual of mental
disorders* (Text rev., 4th ed.). Washington,
DC: Author.

American Psychiatric Association. (2013).
*Diagnostic and statistical manual of mental
disorders* (5th ed.). Washington, DC: Author.

Asperger, H. (1944). Die 'autistischen psychopathen' im kindesalter. *Archiv für Psychiatrie und Nervenkrankheiten, 117,* 76–136.

Attwood, T. (1996). *Asperger's syndrome: A guide for parents and professionals.* Philadelphia, PA: Jessica Kingsley.

Attwood, T. (2004). Cognitive behaviour therapy for children and adults with Asperger's syndrome. *Behaviour Change, 21,* 147–161.

Autism Speaks. (2013). *Leading the way: Autism-friendly youth organization guide.* Retrieved from http://www.autismspeaks.org/sites/default/files/autism_friendly_youth_organizations.pdf

Baker, J. (2001). *The social skills picture book: Teaching play, emotion and communication to children with autism.* Arlington, TX: Future Horizons.

Baron-Cohen, S., O'Riordan, M., Stone, V., Jones, R., & Plaisted, K. (1999). Recognition of faux pas by normally developing children and children with Asperger's syndrome or high-functioning autism. *Journal of Autism and Developmental Disorders, 29,* 407–418.

Board of Education of Hendrick Hudson Central School District, Westchester City v. Rowley, 458 U.S. 176 (1982).

Bock, M. A. (2001). SODA strategy: Enhancing the social interaction skills of youngsters. *Intervention in School and Clinic, 36,* 272–278.

Bolick, T. (2001). *Asperger's syndrome and adolescence: Helping teens get ready for the real world.* Gloucester, MA: Fair Winds Press.

Cannon, L., Kenworthy, L., Alexander, K., & Anthony, L. (2011). *Unstuck and on target!: An executive function curriculum to improve flexibility for children with autism spectrum disorders.* Baltimore, MD: Brookes.

Cederlund, M., Hagberg, B., Billstedt, E., Gillberg, I. C., & Gillberg, C. (2008). Asperger syndrome and autism: A comparative longitudinal follow-up study more than 5 years after original diagnosis. *Journal of Autism and Developmental Disorders, 38,* 72–85.

Centers for Disease Control and Prevention. (2012). Prevalence of autism spectrum disorders—Autism and Developmental Disabilities Monitoring Network, 14 sites, United States, 2008. *Morbidity and Mortality Weekly Report Surveillance Summaries, 61,* 1–18.

Centers for Disease Control and Prevention. (n.d.). *Prevalence of the autism spectrum disorders in multiple areas of the United States, surveillance years 2000 and 2002: A report from the autism and developmental disabilities monitoring (ADDM) network.* Retrieved from http://www.cdc.gov/ncbddd/dd/addmprevalence.htm

Charman, T., Howlin, P., Berry, B., & Prince, E. (2004). Measuring developmental progress of children with autistic spectrum disorder on school entry using parental report. *Autism, 8,* 89–100.

Christensen, J., Grønborg, T. K., Sørensen, M. J., Schendel, D., Parner, E. T., Pederson, L. H., & Vestergaard, M. (2013). Prenatal valproate exposure and risk of autism spectrum disorders and childhood autism. *Journal of the American Medical Association, 309,* 1696–1703.

Constantino, J. N., & Todd, R. D. (2003). Autistic traits in the general population: A twin study. *Archives of General Psychiatry, 60,* 524–530.

Coucouvanis, J. (2005). *Super skills: A social skills program for students with Asperger's syndrome, high functioning autism and related challenges.* Shawnee Mission, KS: Autism Asperger's.

Critchley, H. D., Daly, E. M., Bullmore, E. T., Williams, S., Van Amelsvoort, T., Robertson, D. M., . . . Murphy, D. G. M. (2000). The functional neuroanatomy of social behaviour: Changes in cerebral blood flow when people with autistic disorder process facial expressions. *Brain, 123,* 2203–2212.

Dawson, G., & Burner, K. (2011). Behavioral interventions in children and adolescents with autism spectrum disorder: A review of recent findings. *Current Opinion in Pediatrics, 23,* 616–620.

Denckla, M. (1994). Measurement of executive function. In G. R. Lyon (Ed.), *Frames of reference for the assessment of learning disabilities: New views on measurement issues* (pp. 117–142). Baltimore, MD: Brookes.

Dennis, E. L., & Thompson, P. M. (2013). Typical and atypical brain development: A review of neuroimaging studies. *Dialogues Clinical Neuroscience, 15,* 359–384.

Dichter, G. S. (2012). Functional magnetic resonance imaging of autism spectrum disorders. *Dialogues Clinical Neuroscience, 14,* 319–351.

Durkin, M. S., Maenner, M. J., Meaney, F. J., Levy, S. E., DiGuiseppi, C., Nicholas, J. S. . . . Schieve, L. A. (2010). Socioeconomic inequality in the prevalence of autism spectrum disorder: evidence from a U.S. cross-sectional study. *Plos One, 5,* e11551.

Engström, I., Ekström, L., & Emilsson, B. (2003). Psychosocial functioning in a group of Swedish adults with Asperger's syndrome or high-functioning autism. *Autism, 7,* 99–110.

Farley, M., McMahon, W., Fombonne, E., Jenson, W., Miller, J., Gardner, M., . . . Coon, H. (2009). Twenty-year outcome for individuals with autism and average or near-average cognitive abilities. *Autism Research, 2,* 109–118.

Fein, D., Barton, M., Eigst, I., Kelley, E., Naigles, L., Schultz, R. T., . . . Tyson, K. (2013). Optimal outcome in individuals with a history of autism. *Journal of Child Psychology and Psychiatry, 54,* 195–205.

Ferentino, S. C. (1991). Teaching social skills to preschool children in a special education program. *Dissertation Abstracts International, 52*(08B), 223–4490.

Fombonne, E. (2003). Epidemiological surveys of autism and other pervasive developmental disorders: An update. *Journal of Autism and Developmental Disorders, 33,* 365–382.

Fombonne, E., Zakarian, R., Bennett, A., Meng, L., & McLean-Heywood, D. (2006). Pervasive developmental disorders in Montreal, Quebec, Canada: Prevalence and links with immunizations. *Pediatrics, 118,* 139–150.

Frith, U. (1991). Asperger and his syndrome. In U. Frith (Ed.), *Autism and Asperger's syndrome* (pp. 1–36). Cambridge, UK: Cambridge University Press.

Gerhardt, P. (2012). *Evidence-based practices and transitioning for adolescent and adults with ASD: Implication for quality of life.* Workshop presented in Rockville, MD.

Geschwind, D. H. (2011). Genetics of autism spectrum disorders. *Trends in Cognitive Sciences, 15,* 409–416.

Gillham, J. E., Carter, A. S., Volkmar, F. R., & Sparrow, S. S. (2000). Toward a developmental operational definition of autism. *Journal of Autism and Developmental Disorders, 30,* 269–278.

Goldstein, G., Allen, D. N., Minshew, N. J., Williams, D. L., Volkmar, F., Klin, A., & Schultz, R. J. (2008). The structure of intelligence in children and adults with high functioning autism. *Neuropsychology, 22,* 301–312.

Grandin, T., & Duffy, K. (2004). *Developing talents: Careers for individuals with Asperger's syndrome and high-functioning autism.* Shawnee Mission, KS: Autism Asperger's.

Grandin, T., & Duffy, K. (2008). *Developing talents: Careers for individuals with Asperger's syndrome and high-functioning autism* (Updated ed.). Shawnee Mission, KS: Autism Asperger's.

Gray, C. (2000). *The new social story book.* Arlington, TX: Future Horizons.

Gray, C., & White, A. L. (Eds.). (2002). *My social stories book.* New York, NY: Jessica Kingsley.

Griswold, D. E., Barnhill, G. P., Myles, B. S., Hagiwara, T., & Simpson, R. L. (2002). Asperger's syndrome and academic achievement. *Focus on Autism and Other Developmental Disabilities, 17,* 94–102.

Guglielmo, H. M., & Tryon, G. S. (2001). Social skill training in an integrated preschool program. *School Psychology Quarterly, 16,* 158–175.

Happé, F. (2011). Criteria, categories, and continua: Autism and related disorders in DSM-5. *Journal of the American Academy of Child and Adolescent Psychiatry, 50,* 540–542.

Hill, E. (2004). Executive dysfunction in autism. *Trends in Cognitive Sciences, 8,* 26–32.

Howlin, P., Goode, S., Hutton, J., & Rutter, M. (2004). Adult outcome for children with autism. *Journal of Adult Psychiatry, 45,* 212–229.

Howlin, P., & Moss, P. (2012). Adults with autism spectrum disorders. *Canadian Journal of Psychiatry, 57,* 275–283.

Hultman, C. M., Sandin, S., Levine, S. Z., Lichtenstein, P., & Reichenberg, A. (2010). Advancing paternal age and risk of autism: New evidence from a population-based study and a meta-analysis of epidemiological studies. *Molecular Psychiatry, 16,* 1203–1212.

Individuals with Disabilities Education Act, 20 U.S.C. € 1401 et seq. (1990).

Individual with Disabilities Education Improvement Act, 34 CFR C.F.R. € 300 and 301 (2006).

Iseman, J. S., Silverman, S. M., & Jeweler, S. (2010). *101 school success tools for students with ADHD.* Waco, TX: Prufrock Press.

J. L., M. L. and K. L. v. Mercer Island School District (W.D. WA 2006).

Jensen, P. S., Hinshaw, S. P., & Swanson, J. M. (2001). Findings from the NIMH Multimodal Treatment Study of ADHD (MTA): Implications and applications for primary care providers. *Developmental and Behavioral Pediatrics, 22,* 60–73.

Johnson, S. A. (2004). Social processing in Asperger's disorder. *Dissertation Abstracts International, 64*(7-B), 3552.

Kaland, N., Moller-Nielsen, A., Callesen, K., Mortensen, E. L., Gottlieb, D., & Smith, L. (2002). New "advanced" test of theory of mind: Evidence of children and adolescents with Asperger's syndrome. *Journal of Child Psychology and Psychiatry, 43*, 517–528.

Kanner, L. (1943). Autistic disturbances of affective contact. *Nervous Child, 2*, 217–250.

Kanner, L., & Eisenberg, L. (1956). Early infantile autism 1943–1955. *American Journal of Orthopsychiatry, 26*, 55–65.

Kasari, C., & Lawton, K. (2010). New directions in behavioral treatment of autism spectrum disorders. *Current Opinion in Neurology, 23*, 137–143.

Kasari, C., & Rotheram-Fuller, E. (2005). Current trends in psychological research on children with high-functioning autism and Asperger disorder. *Current Opinion in Psychiatry, 18*, 497–501.

Kenworthy, L. (2011). Asperger's syndrome. In J. E. Morgan, I. S. Baron, & J. Ricker (Eds.), *Casebook of clinical neuropsychology* (pp. 18–27). London, England: Oxford University Press.

Kenworthy, L., & Anthony, L. G. (2012). Understanding and using neurocognitive assessment results in children with neurodevelopmental disabilities. In M. L. Batshaw, N. Roizen, G. Lotrecchiano (Eds.), *Children with disabilities* (7th ed., pp. 267–290). Baltimore, MD: Brookes.

Kenworthy, L., Anthony, L. G., Alexander, K. C., Werner, M. A., Cannon, L., & Greenman, L. (2014). *Unstuck and on target everywhere: Teaching executive functions in everyday life.* Baltimore, MD: Brookes.

Kenworthy, L. E., Black, D. O., Wallace, G. L., Ahluvalia, T., Wagner, A. E., & Sirian, L. M. (2005). Disorganization: The forgotten executive dysfunction in high functioning autism (HFA) spectrum disorders. *Developmental Neuropsychology, 28*, 809–827.

Kenworthy, L., Case, L., Harms, M., Martin, A., & Wallace, G. L. (2009). Adaptive behavior ratings correlate with symptomatology and IQ among adolescents with high-functioning autism spectrum disorders. *Journal of Autism Developmental Disorders, 40,* 416–423.

Kenworthy, L., Yerys, B. E., Anthony, L., & Wallace, G. L. (2008). Understanding executive control in autism spectrum disorders in the lab and in the real world. *Neuropsychology Review, 18,* 320–338.

Kenworthy, L., Yerys, B. E., Weinblatt, R., Abrams, D. N., & Wallace, G. L. (2013). Motor demands impact speed of information processing in autism spectrum disorders. *Neuropsychology, 27,* 529–536. doi:10.1037/a0033599

Klin, A., Jones, W., Schultz, R., & Volkmar, F. (2003). The enactive mind, or from actions to cognition: Lessons from autism. *Philosophical Transactions of the Royal Society B: Biological Sciences, 28,* 345–360.

Klin, A., Saulnier, C. A., Sparrow, S. S., Cicchetti, D. V., Volkmar, F. R., & Lord, C. (2007). Social and communication abilities and disabilities in higher functioning individuals with autism spectrum disorders: The Vineland and the ADOS. *Journal of Autism and Developmental Disorders, 37,* 748–759.

Klin, A., Volkmar, F. R., & Sparrow, S. S. (2000). *Asperger's syndrome.* New York, NY: Guilford.

Lang, R., Regester, A., Lauderdale, S., Asbaugh, K., & Haring, A. (2010). Treatment of anxiety in autism spectrum disorders using cognitive behaviour therapy: A systematic review. *Developmental Neurorehabilitation, 13,* 53–63.

Leyfer, O. T., Folstein, S. E., Bacalman, S., Davis, N. O., Dinh, E., Morgan, J., . . . Lainhart, J. E. (2006). Comorbid psychiatric disorders in children with autism: Interview development and rates of disorders. *Journal of Autism and Developmental Disorders, 36,* 849–861.

Little, L. (2002). Middle-class mothers' perceptions of peer and sibling victimization among children with Asperger's syndrome and nonverbal learning disorders. *Issues in Comprehensive Pediatric Nursing, 25,* 43–57.

Lord, C., Petkova, E., Hus, V., Gan, W., Lu, F., Martin, D. M., ... Risi, S. (2012). A multisite study of the clinical diagnosis of different autism spectrum disorders. *Archives of General Psychiatry, 69,* 306–313.

Loukusa, S., & Moilanen, I. (2009). Pragmatic inference abilities in individuals with Asperger's syndrome or high-functioning autism. A review. *Research in Autism Spectrum Disorders, 3,* 890–904.

MacNeil, L. K., & Mostofsky, S. H. (2012). Specificity of dyspraxia in children with autism. *Neuropsychology, 26,* 165–171. doi:10.1037/a0026955

Madrigal, S., & Winner, M. G. (2008). *Superflex: A social thinking curriculum.* San Jose, CA: Think Social.

Magnusen, C. L., & Attwood, T. (2005). *Teaching children with autism and related spectrum disorders: An art and a science.* Philadelphia, PA: Jessica Kingsley.

Marks, S. U., Schrader, C., Levine, M., Hagie, C., Longaker, T., Morales, M., & Peters, I. (1999). Social skills for social ills: Supporting the social skills development of adolescents with Asperger's syndrome. *Teaching Exceptional Children, 32*(2), 56–61.

Marriage, S., Wolverton, A., & Marriage, K. (2009). Autism spectrum disorder grown up: A chart review of adult functioning. *Journal of the Canadian Academy of Child and Adolescent Psychiatry, 18,* 322–328.

Marston, G. M., & Clarke, D. J. (1999). Making contact: Bereavement and Asperger's syndrome. *Irish Journal of Psychological Medicine, 16,* 29–31.

Mayes, S. D., & Calhoun, S. L. (2008). WISC-IV and WIAT-II profiles in children with high-functioning autism. *Journal of Autism and Developmental Disorders, 38,* 428–439.

Mazurek, M., & Engelhardt, C. (2013). Video game use and problem behaviors in boys with autism spectrum disorders. *Research in Autism Spectrum Disorders, 7,* 316–324.

McConachie, H., Le Couteur, A., & Honey, E. (2005). Can a diagnosis of Asperger's syndrome be made in very young children with suspected autism spectrum disorder? *Journal of Autism and Developmental Disorders, 35,* 167–176.

Meyer, R. N., & Attwood, T. (2001). *Asperger's syndrome employment workbook: An employment workbook for adults with Asperger's syndrome.* Philadelphia, PA: Jessica Kingsley.

Monahan, M., & Classen, S. (2013). Best practices in promoting drivers' education to enhance participation. In G. Frolek-Clark & B. Chandler (Eds.), *Best practices in school-based occupational therapy* (pp. 561–572). Bethesda, MD: AOTA Press.

Monroe, S. J. (2007). *Dear colleague letter: Access by students with disabilities to challenging academic programs.* Retrieved from http://www2.ed.gov/about/offices/list/ocer/letters/colleague-20071226.html

Morton, O. (2001, December). Think different? Autism researcher Simon Baron-Cohen on "mindblind" engineers, hidden pictures, and a future designed for people with Asperger's [Electronic version]. *Wired, 9.* Retrieved from http://www.wired.com/wired/archive/9.12/baron-cohen.html

Mottron, L. (2004). Matching strategies in cognitive research with individuals with high-functioning autism: Current practices, instrument biases, and recommendations. *Journal of Autism and Developmental Disorders, 34,* 19–27.

Moyes, R. A. (2002). *Addressing the challenging behavior of children with high-functioning autism/Asperger's syndrome in the classroom: A guide for teachers and parents.* Philadelphia, PA: Jessica Kingsley.

Mr. and Mrs. I. vs. Maine School Administrative District No. 55, 04-165-P-H (U. S. District Court, Maine, 2006).

Musgrove, M. (2013). *Dear colleague letter on bullying.* Retrieved from http://www.ed.gov/blog/2013/08/keeping-students-with-disabilities-safe-from-bullying/

Myles, B. S., & Adreon, D. (2001). *Asperger's syndrome and adolescence: Practical solutions for school success.* Shawnee Mission, KS: Autism Asperger's.

Myles, B. S., & Simpson, R. L. (1998). *Asperger's syndrome: A guide for educators and parents.* Austin, TX: PRO-ED.

Myles, B. S., & Southwick, J. (1999). *Asperger's syndrome and difficult moments: Practical solutions for tantrums, rage, and meltdowns.* Shawnee Mission, KS: Autism Asperger's.

Nash, J. M. (2002, May 6). The secrets of autism [Electronic version]. *TIME.* Retrieved from http://www.time.com/time/magazine/article/0,9171,1002364-1,00.html

Neu, T. W., & Weinfeld, R. (2006). *Helping boys succeed in school: A practical guide for parents and teachers.* Waco, TX: Prufrock Press.

Notbohm, E., & Zysk, V. (2010). *1001 great ideas for teaching & raising children with autism or Asperger's* (2nd ed.). Arlington, TX: Future Horizons.

Oliveras-Rentas, R., Kenworthy, L., Roberson, R. B., Martin, A., & Wallace, G. L. (2012). WISC-IV profile in high-functioning autism spectrum disorders: impaired processing speed is associated with increased autism communication symptoms and decreased adaptive communication abilities. *Journal of Autism and Developmental Disorders, 42,* 655–664.

Olmstead v. L. C. (98-536) 527 U.S. 581 (1999)138 F.3d 893.

Ozonoff, S., Garcia, N., Clark, E., & Lainhart, J. (2005). MMPI-2 personality profiles of high-functioning adults with autism spectrum disorders. *Assessment, 12,* 86–95.

Palmer, A. (2006). *Realizing the college dream with autism or Asperger's syndrome: A parent's guide to student success.* New York, NY: Jessica Kingsley.

Persico, A. M., & Napolioni, V. (2013). Autism genetics. *Behavioural Brain Research, 251,* 95–112.

Powers, M. D., & Poland, J. (2003). *Asperger's syndrome and your child: A parent's guide.* New York, NY: HarperCollins.

Price, J., & Fisher, J. (2010). *Take control of Asperger's syndrome: The official strategy guide for teens with Asperger's syndrome and nonverbal learning disorder.* Waco, TX: Prufrock Press.

Ralabate, P. (Ed.). (2006). *The puzzle of autism.* Washington, DC: National Education Association. Retrieved from http://www.nea.org/specialed/images/autismpuzzle.pdf

Roberts, A. L., Lyall, K., Hart, J. E., Laden, F., Just, A. C., Bobb, J. F., Koenen, K. C., . . . Weisskopf, M. G. (2013). Perinatal air pollutant exposures and autism spectrum disorder in the children of nurses' health study II participants. *Environmental Health Perspectives, 121,* 978–984.

Robison, J. E. (2008). *Look me in the eye: My life with Asperger's.* New York, NY: Crown.

Robison, J. E. (2011). *Authors @ Google: John Elder Robison.* Retrieved from http://www.youtube.com/watch?v=2QeFAeWqYp4

Robison, J. (2012). *Be different: My adventures with Asperger's and my advice for fellow Aspergerians, misfits, families, and teachers.* New York, NY: Broadway.

Rose, D. H., & Gravel, J. W. (2010). Universal design for learning. In E. Baker, P. Peterson, & B. McGaw (Eds.), *International encyclopedia of education* (3rd ed., pp. 119–124). Oxford, England: Elsevier.

Rourke, B. P., & Tsatsanis, K. D. (2000). Nonverbal learning disabilities. In A. Klin, F. R. Volkmar, & S. S. Sparrow (Eds.), *Asperger's syndrome* (pp. 231–253). New York, NY: Guilford.

Russell, E., & Sofronoff, K. (2005). Anxiety and social worries in children with Asperger's syndrome. *Australian and New Zealand Journal of Psychiatry, 39,* 633–638.

Schultz, R. T., Gauthier, I., Klin, A., Fulbright, R. K., Anderson, A. W., Volkmar, F., . . . Gore, J. C. (2000). Abnormal ventral temporal cortical activity during face discrimination among individuals with autism and Asperger's syndrome. *Archives of General Psychiatry, 57,* 331–340.

Shapiro, D. (2006, August). *ADHD review*. Lecture presented at Siena School, Silver Spring, MD.

Shelton, J. F., Hertz-Picciotto, I., & Pessah, I. N. (2012). Tipping the balance of autism risk: Potential mechanisms linking pesticides and autism. *Environmental Health Perspectives, 120*, 944–951.

Silverman, S. M., Iseman, J. S., & Jeweler, S. (2009). *School success for kids with ADHD*. Waco, TX: Prufrock Press.

Silverman, S. M., & Weinfeld, R. (2007). *School success for kids with Asperger's syndrome*. Waco, TX: Prufrock Press.

Smith, L. E., Maenner, M. J., & Seltzer, M. M. (2012). Developmental trajectories in adolescents and adults with autism: The case of daily living skills. *Journal of the American Academy of Child and Adolescent Psychiatry, 51*, 622–631.

Stokes, M., Newton, N., & Kaur, A. (2007). Stalking, and social and romantic functioning among adolescents and adults with autism spectrum disorder. *Journal of Autism and Developmental Disorders, 37*, 1969–1986.

Suckling, A., & Temple, C. (2001). *Bullying: A whole-school approach*. Philadelphia, PA: Jessica Kingsley.

Szatmari, P. (2000). The classification of autism, Asperger's syndrome, and pervasive developmental disorder. *Canadian Journal of Psychiatry, 45*, 731–738.

Tantam, D. (2000). Psychological disorder in adolescents and adults with Asperger's syndrome. *Autism, 4*, 47–62.

Taylor, J. L., & Seltzer, M. M. (2010). Changes in the autism behavioral phenotype during the transition to adulthood. *Journal of Autism and Developmental Disorders, 40*, 1431–1446.

Tomlinson, C. A. (1999). *The differentiated classroom: Responding to the needs of all learners*. Alexandria, VA: Association for Supervision and Curriculum Development.

Toth, K., & King, B. H. (2008). Asperger's syndrome: Diagnosis and treatment. *American Journal of Psychiatry, 165*, 958–963.

U.S. Department of Education. (2013, February). *Social skills training* (What Works Clearinghouse intervention report). Retrieved from http://ies.ed.gov/ncee/wwc/pdf/intervention_reports/wwc_socialskills_020513.pdf

Volkmar, F. R., & Klin, A. (1998). Asperger's syndrome and nonverbal learning disabilities. In E. Schopler, G. B. Mesibov, & L. J. Kunce (Eds.), *Asperger's syndrome or high-functioning autism?* (pp. 107–121). New York, NY: Plenum Press.

Wachtel, L. E., & Shorter, E. (2013). Autism plus psychosis: A 'one-two punch' risk for tragic violence? *Medical Hypotheses, 81,* 404–409.

Wallace, G. L., Silvers, J. A., Martin, A., & Kenworthy, L. (2009). Brief report: Further evidence for inner speech deficits in autism spectrum disorders. *Journal of Autism Developmental Disorders, 39,* 1735–1739.

Weinfeld, R., Barnes-Robinson, L., Jeweler, S., & Roffman Shevitz, B. (2013). *Smart kids with learning difficulties: Overcoming obstacles and realizing potential* (2nd ed.). Waco, TX: Prufrock Press.

Weinfeld, R., & Davis, M. (2008). *Special needs advocacy resource book: What you can do now to advocate for your exceptional child's education.* Waco, TX: Prufrock Press.

Williams, E. (2004). Who really needs "theory" of mind? An interpretative phenomenological analysis of the autobiographical writings of ten high-functioning individuals with an autism spectrum disorder. *Theory & Psychology, 14,* 704–724.

Winner, M. G. (2013). *The social communication dance: The four communication steps.* Retrieved from https://www.socialthinking.com/what-is-social-thinking/published-articles/198-the-social-communication-dance-the-four-steps-of-communication

Williams, M. S., & Shellenberger, S. (1996). *How does your engine run? A leader's guide to the alert program for self-regulation.* Albuquerque, NM: Therapyworks.

Wing, L. (1981). Asperger's syndrome: A clinical account. *Psychological Medicine, 11,* 115–129.

Zafeiriou, D. I., Ververi, A., Dafoulis, V., Kalyva, E., & Vargiami, E. (2013). Autism spectrum disorders: The quest for genetic syndromes. *American Journal of Medical Genetics, 162B*, 327–366.

Zerbo, O., Iosif, A., Walker, C., Ozonoff, S., Hansen, R. L., & Hertz-Picciotto, I. (2013). Is maternal influenza or fever during pregnancy associated with autism or developmental delays? Results from the CHARGE (CHildhood Autism Risks from Genetics and Environment) study. *Journal of Autism and Developmental Disorders, 43*, 25–33.

Zucker, B. (2008). *Anxiety-free kids: An interactive guide for parents and children.* Waco, TX: Prufrock Press.

Resources

National Organizations

ASPEN
9 Aspen Circle
Edison, NJ 08820
Phone: (732) 321-0880
E-mail: info@AspenNJ.org
Website: http://www.aspennj.org

Asperger's Association of New England (AANE)
51 Water Street, Suite 206
Watertown, MA 02472
Phone: (617) 393-3824
E-mail: info@aane.org
Website: http://aane.autistics.org

Autism Network International (ANI)
P.O. Box 35448
Syracuse, NY 13235-5448
E-mail: jisincla@mailbox.syr.edu
Website: http://ani.autistics.org

Autism Research Institute (ARI)
4182 Adams Avenue
San Diego, CA 92116
Phone: (619) 281-7165
Website: http://www.autism.com

Autism Resource Network
5757 Sanibel Drive
Minnetonka, MN 55343
Phone (952) 988-0088
E-mail: info@autismshop.com
Website: http://www.autismshop.com

Autism Society of America (ASA)
4340 East-West Hwy, Suite 350
Bethesda, MD 20814-3067
Phone: (301) 657-0881
Website: http://www.autism-society.org

Autism Society of North Carolina
505 Oberlin Road, Ste. 230
Raleigh, NC 27605-1345
Phone: (919) 743-0204
E-mail: info@autismsociety-nc.org
Website: http://www.autismsociety-nc.org

Autism Speaks
1 East 33rd Street, 4th Floor
New York, NY 10016
Phone: (212) 252-8584
E-mail: contactus@autismspeaks.org
Website: http://www.autismspeaks.org

Council For Exceptional Children
2900 Crystal Drive, Ste. 1000
Arlington, VA 22202-3557
Phone: (703) 620-3660; (888) 232-7733
Website: http://www.cec.sped.org

Future Horizons
721 W. Abram Street
Arlington, TX 76013
Phone: (800) 489-0727
Website: http://www.FHautism.com

Kennedy Krieger Institute
707 North Broadway
Baltimore, MD 21205
Phone: (800) 873-3377
E-mail: info@kennedykrieger.org
Website: http://www.kennedykrieger.org

Learning Disabilities Association of America (LDA)
4156 Library Road
Pittsburgh, PA 15234-1349
Phone: (412) 341-1515
Website: http://www.ldanatl.org

MAAP Services for Autism & Asperger's Syndrome
P.O. Box 524
Crown Point, IN 46308
Phone: (219) 662-1311
E-mail: info@maapservices.org
Website: http://www.aspergerssyndrome.org

M.I.N.D. Institute
2825 50th Street
Sacramento, CA 95817
Phone: (916) 703-0280
Website: http://www.ucdmc.ucdavis.edu/mindinstitute

National Autism Center
41 Pacella Park Drive
Randolph, MA 02368
Phone: (877) 313-3833
E-mail: info@nationalautismcenter.org
Website: http://www.nationalautismcenter.org

National Institute of Mental Health (NIMH)
6001 Executive Blvd., Rm. 8184, MSC 9663
Bethesda, MD 20892-9663
Phone: (866) 615-6464
E-mail: nimhinfo@nih.gov
Website: http://www.nimh.nih.gov

Unlocking Autism
P.O. Box 209
Tyrone, GA 30290
Phone: (866) 366-3361
Website: www.unlockingautism.org

Yale University Child Study Center
230 South Frontage Rd.
New Haven, CT 06519
Phone: (203) 785-2540
Website: http://childstudycenter.yale.edu

Websites

Asperger's Info.com
   http://www.Aspergersinfo.com

Asperger's Planet
   http://www.Aspergersplanet.com

Autism Link
   http://www.autismlink.com

Asperger's Disorder Homepage
   http://www.Aspergers.com

Autism Resources Page
   http://www.autism-resources.com

Center for the Study of Autism
   http://www.globalautismcollaboration.com

Do2Learn
   http://Do2Learn.com

Education Law Center
   http://www.edlawcenter.org

The Global and Regional Asperger's Syndrome Partnership
(GRASP)
   http://www.grasp.org

K–12 Academics
   http://k12academics.com/Aspergers.htm

National Center to Improve Practice in Special Education Through Technology, Media and Materials (NCIP)
http://www2.edc.org/NCIP

Online Asperger's Syndrome Information and Support (OASIS)
http://www.Aspergersyndrome.org

Tony Attwood's website
http://www.tonyattwood.com.au

University of Michigan Health System Autism and Pervasive Developmental Disorders
http://www.med.umich.edu/1libr/yourchild/autism.htm

U.S. Department of Education
http://www.ed.gov

Wrightslaw
http://www.wrightslaw.com

Wrong Planet
http://www.wrongplanet.net

Checklist of Issues That Teachers and Parents May Observe in the Classroom

Parents and teachers should utilize this checklist to note issues that they are observing in the classroom for students with HFASD. It can serve as a discussion tool for parent-teacher conferences and 504/IEP meetings.

❑ Problems with social interactions

❑ Problems with flexibility, organization, attention, and other areas of executive functioning

❑ Problems with ritualistic, repetitive, or rigid behavior

❑ Need for predictability

❑ Very focused areas of interest and expertise

❑ Problems with sensory hypo- or hypersensitivity

❑ Problems with language

❑ Problems with abstract reasoning

❑ Problems with motor issues including written production

❑ Problems with anxiety, depression, and emotional regulation

Intervention Plan for Students With HFASD

Teachers and school staff members should use this tool as a way to formulate a school plan for students with HFASD. Fill out Parts 1–3 to analyze what is currently happening with the student and then fill out Parts 4 and 5 to plan what needs to be done.

Name: _____

Date: _____

School: _____

1. **Evidence of Strengths:**
   Test scores:

   Performance in school (When does the student show interest, perseverance, self-regulation, and outstanding achievement?):

   Performance in the community:

2. **Evidence of Learning Challenges:**
   Problems with social interactions:

   Problems with flexibility, organization, attention, and other areas of executive functioning:

   Problems with ritualistic, repetitive, or rigid behavior:

   Need for predictability:

   Very focused areas of interest and expertise:

Problems with sensory hypo- or hypersensitivity:

Problems with language:

Problems with abstract reasoning:

Problems with motor issues including written production:

Problems with anxiety, depression, and emotional regulation:

3. **Current Program:**
    Instruction in the area of strengths (gifted or advanced-level instruction):

    Adaptations:

    Accommodations:

    Special instruction in areas that are affected by the disability:
        Problems with social interactions:

        Problems with flexibility, organization, attention, and other areas of
        executive functioning:

Problems with ritualistic, repetitive, or rigid behavior:

Need for predictability:

Very focused areas of interest and expertise:

Problems with sensory hypo- or hypersensitivity:

Problems with language:

Problems with abstract reasoning:

Problems with motor issues including written production:

Problems with anxiety, depression, and emotional regulation:

Case management (communication between home and school and among staff):

4. **Recommendations:**

Strength-based instruction:

Adaptations:

Accommodations:

Special instruction in the areas affected by the disability:
    Problems with social interactions:

    Problems with flexibility, organization, attention, and other areas of executive functioning:

    Problems with ritualistic, repetitive, or rigid behavior:

    Need for predictability:

    Very focused areas of interest and expertise:

    Problems with sensory hypo- or hypersensitivity:

Problems with language:

Problems with abstract reasoning:

Problems with motor issues including written production:

Problems with anxiety, depression, and emotional regulation:

Case management:

5. Next steps:

Note. Adapted from *Smart Kids With Learning Difficulties: Overcoming Obstacles and Realizing Potential* (2nd ed., pp. 235–237), by R. Weinfeld, L. Barnes-Robinson, S. Jeweler, and B. Roffman Shevitz, 2013, Waco, TX: Prufrock Press. Copyright © 2013 Prufrock Press.

Quick Reference to Problem Areas and Interventions

Strategies and Interventions That Work With Social Interactions

- » Protect students from bullying and teasing
- » Educate other students about HFASD and about the child's unique strengths and challenges
- » Utilize strengths and interests in cooperative learning
- » Teach theory of mind: Learning to understand the perspectives, feelings, and thoughts of others
- » Teach students how to read and react to nonverbal social cues
- » Teach students how to participate in conversations
- » Teach students to identify, understand, and cope with emotions

Strategies or Interventions That Work to Deal With Flexibility, Organization, Attention, and Other Areas of Executive Functioning

» Provide direct instruction in executive function skills
» Use visual schedules
» Use proximity to and prompting from the teacher
» Structure work periods
» Structure the environment
» Utilize visual supports that aid with completion of assignments
» Support organization with rubrics, study guides, and outlines
» Provide classroom structures that support organization of materials
» Utilize technology
» Provide systematic supports for organizational help
» Structure time during the school day for organization of assignments and materials

Strategies and Interventions That Work to Deal With Ritualistic, Repetitive, or Rigid Behavior

» Tackle rigid behavior by explicitly teaching flexibility
» Conduct a Functional Behavioral Analysis (FBA) and develop a Behavior Intervention Plan (BIP)
» If possible, intervene before the behavior becomes established, distracting, or disruptive
» Respond to behaviors in a way that will help minimize the impact of the behavior and/or extinguish it

Strategies and Interventions That Work to Provide Predictability

» Provide clear rules and consequences
» Provide clear physical structure in the classroom

» Provide a clear physical schedule in the classroom
» Prepare for changes and transitions
» Provide structure for unstructured time
» Provide instruction about the hidden curriculum

Strategies and Interventions That Work With Very Focused Areas of Interest and Expertise

» Provide a specific time of the day for focus on the area of interest
» Help students develop their area of interest and relate it to future employment
» Use the special area of interest as a bridge to other topics
» Use the area of interest as a way to facilitate social interaction
» Use the student's area of interest to help regulate behavior

Strategies or Interventions That Work to Deal With Sensory Hyper- and Hyposensitivity

» Alter or change the environment to decrease factors to which the student may be hyper- or hyposensitive
» Work proactively to prepare the student to deal with his issues around hypo- and hypersensitivity
» Employ strategies that serve to help the students to calm or alert themselves

Strategies and Interventions That Work for Problems With Language

» Avoid or carefully explain ambiguous language such as idioms, metaphors, phrasal verbs, and figures of speech
» Avoid or explain the use of sarcasm or jokes with double meanings
» Avoid or explain the use of nicknames

» Teach students how to find key words and concepts in directions and instructions

Strategies or Interventions That Work to Improve Abstract Reasoning

» Break down the goal of the lesson into its component parts and provide supports
» Utilize "naturalistic" instruction
» Provide appropriate accommodations throughout instruction
» Provide adaptations to the way the lesson will be taught
» Provide explicit instruction to ensure understanding of the concept being taught
» Move from specifics to generalizations
» Provide alternative ways for students to demonstrate understanding that allow them to utilize their strengths

Strategies and Interventions That Work to Deal With Motor Issues Including Written Production

» Provide support with and alternatives to physical education and recess
» Provide support in acquiring written language skills
» Provide tools that allow for improvement of handwriting
» Provide alternatives that allow students to write more easily or circumvent writing
» Allow and encourage students to use technology as an alternative to handwriting

Strategies or Interventions That Work With Anxiety, Depression, and Emotional Regulation

» Work to proactively minimize situations that will cause emotional problems

» Identify signs of stress and/or overstimulation early and intervene before the problem becomes overwhelming
» Allow and encourage students to employ techniques that will allow for self-calming and regaining emotional control
» Allow students to move to a special area in the classroom or building
» Help students to gain skills in monitoring and responding to their own behavior
» Teach students to prepare for stressful, overstimulating, and uncomfortable situations
» Consider medication with a psychiatrist or pediatrician
» Consider behavioral consultation with a behavior intervention specialist

Program Options for Students With HFASD

Parents and teachers can utilize this checklist for gathering information about the educational options available for a student with HFASD.

❑   Instruction in regular classes

Options: _____

_____

_____

_____

_____

_____

_____

❑   Instruction in special classes

Options: _____

_____

_____

_____

_____

_____

❑   Special schools

Options: _____

_____

_____

_____

_____

_____

❑   Alternative school programs

Options: _____

_____

_____

_____

_____

_____

_____

❑   Homeschooling

Options: _____

_____

_____

_____

_____

_____

❑   Home and hospital teaching

Options: _____

_____

_____

_____

_____

_____

Independent Living and World of Work and Resources

» **Independent Living Centers** (http://www.ncil.org) offer assistance in arranging for disability-related benefits and services for people with disabilities to live independently in their communities, including personal assistance services, transportation, housing, and benefits planning.

» **The Vocational Rehabilitation program** (http://www.ed.gov/about/offices/list/osers/rsa/index.html) provides a wide range of services and job training to people with disabilities who want to work.

» **Healthy and Ready to Work** (http://www.hrtw.org) provides information for youth with disabilities and their families to maximize their health potential while transitioning from childhood to adulthood.

» **The National Consortium for Health Systems Development** (http://www.nchsd.org) is a state-driven technical assistance center supporting Medicaid Infrastructure Grants and innovation that improves employment policy by facilitating collaboration among local, state, and federal experts.

» **The Center for Workers with Disabilities** (http://www.nasmd.org/disabilities) is a technical assistance center of the American Public Health Administrators Association for states developing or enhancing employment and health-related support programs for working persons with disabilities.

» **DisabilityInfo.gov** (http://www.disability.gov) is the gateway to the federal government's disability-related information and resources.

» **GovBenefits.gov** (http://www.benefits.gov/) is a web-based resource for everyone and includes information on a variety of benefit and assistance programs for veterans, seniors, students, teachers, children, people with disabilities, dependents, disaster victims, farmers, caregivers, job seekers, prospective homeowners, and much more.

Print Resources

» *JAN Employee's Practical Guide to Requesting and Negotiating Reasonable Accommodation Under the ADA* (see http://askjan.org/EeGuide)

» *The Asperger's Syndrome Employment Workbook: An Employment Workbook for Adults With Asperger's Syndrome* (Meyer & Attwood, 2001)

Websites

Wrong Planet
  http://www.wrongplanet.net

Autistic Self Advocacy Network (ASAN)
  http://www.autisticadvocacy.org

Autism Network International (ANI)
  http://www.autreat.com

Job Accommodation Network (JAN)
  http://askjan.org/indiv/index.htm

Equal Employment Opportunity Commission
  http://www.eeoc.gov

Disclosure Decisions: To Get the Job
  http://www.worksupport.com/documents/disclosure%5F
  decisions1%2Epdf

National Workplace Collaborative on Workforce and Disability
  http://www.ncwd-youth.info/411-on-disability-disclosure

EEOC Office List and Jurisdictional Map
  http://www.eeoc.gov/field/index.cfm

Transition Tool Kit Appendix
  http://www.autismspeaks.org/family-services/tool-kits/
  transition-tool-kit/appendix

Social Security Resources

» For information helpful to youth with disabilities and
   their parents, families, teachers, and counselors concern-
   ing Social Security income support benefits and work
   incentives, consult the SSA websites at:
   o http://www.ssa.gov/work
   o http://www.socialsecurity.gov/ssi/spotlights/spot-
      disabled-youth.htm

» To locate a local field office for the Social Security Administration, consult the directory on SSA's website at http://www.ssa.gov.

» Many Social Security field offices have a position known as an Employment Support Representative; this person serves as a technical resource for other SSA employees about disability work programs and services. For more information, go to http://www.ssa.gov/work/index.html.

» SSA currently has three universities responsible for providing core training and technical support to the Benefits Planning Assistance and Outreach program. These include the Benefits Assistance Resource Center at Virginia Commonwealth University (http://www.vcu-ntc.org), the Northeast Work Incentives Support Center at Cornell University (http://www.ilr.cornell.edu/edi/p-wisc.cfm), and the SSA Training and Technical Assistance Center at the University of Missouri at Columbia (http://www.dps.missouri.edu/resources/ssawork/default.html).

» The Ticket-to-Work Program (http://www.yourticketto work.com) offers people with disabilities a "ticket" to obtain the employment support services, vocational rehabilitation services, and other services they may need to get and keep a job.

About the Authors

Stephan M. Silverman, Ph.D., is former Director of Assessment and Behavioral Services for the Weinfeld Education Group. He was a school psychologist in the Montgomery County Public Schools system in Maryland for 30 years and has maintained a private practice in Maryland since 1975. Dr. Silverman earned his B.A. from the University of Maryland and his M.A. and Ph.D. degrees from Emory University. Dr. Silverman was a field trainer for graduate externs and interns in school and clinical psychology for 18 years while working in Montgomery County.

He coauthored *School Success for Kids With Asperger's Syndrome* with Rich Weinfeld. He also coauthored *School Success for Kids With ADHD* and *101 School Success Tools for Students With ADHD* with Dr. Jacqueline Iseman and

Sue Jeweler. He provides training workshops to a wide variety of parent, educator, and professional groups.

Dr. Silverman developed and supervised a multidisciplinary early childhood assessment team focusing on assessment of children from birth through early childhood suspected of autism spectrum disorders. He has worked with children, adolescents, and adults with a wide range of challenges. His practice has emphasized support to parents of children with disabilities and relationships with schools that educate children with disabilities and those who learn differently.

Lauren Kenworthy, Ph.D., is an associate professor of neurology, pediatrics, and psychiatry at the George Washington University School of Medicine and director of the Center for Autism Spectrum Disorders at Children's National Medical Center. She has been on the faculty at Children's National Medical Center and George Washington University School of Medicine since 1995. Dr. Kenworthy's research interests are in the neuropsychology of autism. She is an author of more than 40 peer-reviewed publications documenting nonsocial deficits in autism. She is a coauthor of the Behavior Rating Inventory of Executive Function (BRIEF), which has been used in more than 200 research publications to document executive functioning in various clinical groups. Her recent publications have focused on the role of executive dysfunction in autism and its treatment. She is author of a several books on a school- and home-based executive function intervention for children on the autism spectrum called *Unstuck and On Target!* and is a frequent presenter on autism spectrum disorders and executive functions.

Rich Weinfeld is Director and Founder of Weinfeld Education Group, http://www.weinfeldeducationgroup.com, a group of educational consultants, psychologists, speech-language pathologists, and occupational therapists dedicated to helping all students reach their potential. Rich serves as an expert witness and advocate for appropriate services for students with special needs throughout the United States. The Weinfeld Education

Group also provides training and consultation to school districts, schools, and parent groups.

Rich began his career teaching elementary school and then spent 14 years working with emotionally disturbed students, and 6 years directing a program for students with learning disabilities, physical challenges, and autism spectrum disorders. His career in public school education culminated with 6 years as the director of programs for gifted students with disabilities.

Rich has coauthored six books and many articles on a variety of special needs topics, taught a course on gifted students with disabilities at Johns Hopkins University, created and taught a course on advocacy, and provided training for a wide variety of professionals and parent groups.